Nat Turner
Cry Freedom in America

James T. Baker

THOMSON

™

WADSWORTH

Australia • Canada • Mexico • Singapore • Spain • United Kingdom • United States

Nat Turner
James T. Baker

Custom Editor:
Marc Bove

Project Development Editor:
Greg Albert

Marketing Coordinator:
Sara Mercurio

Production/Manufacturing Supervisor:
Donna M. Brown

Project Coordinator:
Jennifer Atwood

Pre-Media Services Supervisor:
Dan Plofchan

Rights and Permissions Specialist:
Bahman Naraghi

Senior Prepress Specialist:
Deanna Dixon

Printer:
FedEx Kinko's

For information about our products, contact us at:
Thomson Learning Academic Resource Center
(800) 423-0563

For permission to use material from this text or product, submit a request online at **http://www.thomsonrights.com**. Any additional questions about permissions can be submitted by email to
thomsonrights@thomson.com.

The Adaptable Courseware Program consists of products and additions to existing Wadsworth products that are produced from camera-ready copy. Peer review, class testing, and accuracy are primarily the responsibility of the author(s).

Student Edition: ISBN 0-534-61807-3

Thomson Custom Solutions
5191 Natorp Boulevard
Mason, OH 45040
www.thomsoncustom.com

Thomson Higher Education
10 Davis Drive
Belmont, CA 94002-3098
USA

Asia (Including India):
Thomson Learning
60 Albert Street, #15-01
Albert Complex
Singapore 189969
Tel 65 336-6411
Fax 65 336-7411

Australia/New Zealand:
Thomson Learning Australia
102 Dodds Street
Southbank, Victoria 3006
Australia

Latin America:
Thomson Learning
Seneca 53
Colonia Polano
11560 Mexico, D.F., Mexico
Tel (525) 281-2906
Fax (525) 281-2656

Canada:
Thomson Nelson
1120 Birchmount Road
Toronto, Ontario
Canada M1K 5G4
Tel (416) 752-9100
Fax (416) 752-8102

UK/Europe/Middle East/Africa:
Thomson Learning
High Holborn House
50-51 Bedford Row
London, WC1R 4L$
United Kingdom
Tel 44 (020) 7067-2500
Fax 44 (020) 7067-2600

Spain (Includes Portugal):
Thomson Paraninfo
Calle Magallanes 25
28015 Madrid
España
Tel 34 (0)91 446-3350
Fax 34 (0)91 445-6218

To my high school classmates,
who taught me the fun of learning:
Billie Rose, John, Juanez, Carlton, Shirley, Don, Janell,
Leonard, Herb, Charlotte, Marilyn, Jack, Clark, Peggy,
Gerald, Claudene, Sandra, Bennie Nell, Betty, and Virgil.

"I should arise ... and slay my enemies with their own weapons."

Nat Turner, 1831

PREFACE

ABOUT THE SERIES

Nat Turner: Cry Freedom in America, the story of the rebel slave
Nat Turner and his legacy, is the first volume in a series of textbooks
collectively called Creators of the American Mind. Many historians
believe that, despite great diversity among the American people,
there is an American Mind—molded by a common history, common
hopes, common fears—making Americans a distinctive people.
Even when Americans quarrel, the American Mind provides them
with subjects and ammunition for their arguments.

It is the thesis of this series that certain important individuals—
male and female, political, social, religious, and intellectual leaders of
all ethnic groups—have, through their thoughts and deeds, helped
create the American Mind. Americans, whether they admire or
despise these creators, whether they even know of them, reflect in
their own thoughts and deeds these persons. This series will spot-
light some of the creators—listening when possible to their own
words, comparing the sometimes conflicting opinions of their biog-
raphers, juxtaposing their admirers and critics—to show what each
one contributed to the American Mind. Nat Turner, the subject of
this text, is a worthy actor in the great drama of American history
because he is one creator of the American Mind.

ABOUT THIS VOLUME

In 1831, in the third century of slavery in British North America,
thirty-four years before it was ended by the Thirteenth Amendment
to the U.S. Constitution, the slave Nat Turner led a revolt against his
condition in Southampton County, Virginia. His insurrection was
bloody and, in the end, unsuccessful; but it made an indelible
impression on the nation and its history. As late as the 1960s, Turner

and his rebellion were the subjects of a Pulitzer Prize winning novel by William Styron which provoked a major reaction to the novel from irate black writers.

This study of Nat Turner offers a unique approach to his life and the effects of his insurrection on American history. *Nat Turner: Cry Freedom in America*

- presents Nat Turner as a person, not an abstraction but a real flesh-and-blood human being, by letting him speak for himself through the confession (explanation) he made to a scribe just before he died;
- places Nat Turner in historical context by providing
  1. commentary on the nature of slavery by other slaves such as Frederick Douglass and the novelist Harriet Beecher Stowe,
  2. immediate responses to the uprising by contemporaries such as northern abolitionist William Lloyd Garrison and Virginia Governor John Floyd,
  3. perspectives of modern scholars of the subject;
- shows, using documents from Nat Turner's day and from various periods since his death, how his image has changed with successive generations, and how current opinions of him reflect the American Mind in earlier time periods;
- demonstrates how Nat Turner—the man and the myth—still in our day provokes controversy, by presenting excerpts from the Styron novel and reviews of it by both people who praised it and those who condemned it;
- offers more primary sources from more periods of American history than any other study of Nat Turner, giving students an intimate glimpse into the history of slavery and emancipation;
- provides, at appropriate intervals, questions which may be used for in-class discussion or to prompt responsive, reflective essays on the materials;
- includes a list of topics for extended essays or term papers on the materials;
- provides an annotated bibliography so that students may dig deeper than the text itself into the many subjects introduced in the textbook;
- offers ample documents for students to consult in completing a brief research and writing project on slavery, the Nat Turner Revolt, or race relations in America.

While *Nat Turner: Cry Freedom in America* adequately covers this historic story, it is brief enough to be used as a supplementary reader to a larger textbook. It is appropriate for courses such as A Survey of American History, American Social History, Race Relations in America, and African-American History.

ACKNOWLEDGMENTS

The author is grateful to the following reviewers who read this text in manuscript form and made corrective and constructive suggestions on ways to make it more useful to teachers and students: Robert Becker, Louisiana State University; Raymond Hyser, James Madison University; and William Stockton, Johnson County Community College.

Thanks also to the Faculty Research Committee of Western Kentucky University, Elmer Gray Chairman, for providing funds to help bring this project to completion; to Elizabeth Jensen for making it technically presentable; to Drake Bush, David Tatom, and Margaret Beasley of Harcourt Brace College Publishers for their faith and guidance.

CONTENTS

CHRONOLOGY

1619   Arrival of first African slaves in the British colonies

1776   Declaration of Independence says all men are created equal

1789   U.S. Constitution permits states to count each slave as three-fifths of a person

1800   October 2, Nat Turner born in Virginia, a slave of Benjamin Turner

1821   Nat Turner runs away from his master, returning voluntarily after 30 days

1822   Turner is sold to Thomas Moore

1825   Turner receives his first heavenly vision

1828   May 12, Turner receives his second vision

1830   January, Turner is sent to the home of Joseph Travis

1831   August 13, Turner receives his sign from God

       August 21, Turner plans the insurrection

       August 22-23, Turner leads the insurrection

       August 23-October 30, Turner is in hiding, captured at last by Benjamin Phipps

       October 31, Turner is lodged in the Southampton County Jail in Jerusalem, Virginia

       November 1-3, Turner dictates his "Confession" to Thomas R. Gray

       November 5, Turner is tried, found guilty, and sentenced to death

       November 11, Turner is hanged at noon

1838   Fredrick Douglass escapes to freedom

1848   The Crafts escape to freedom; Douglass publishes his most effective critiques of slavery

1852   Harriet Beecher Stowe's *Uncle Tom's Cabin* is published

1861   The Civil War begins, and Thomas Wentworth Higginson publishes a study of Nat Turner

1865   The Thirteenth Amendment to the U.S. Constitution abolishes slavery

1900   William S. Drewry publishes the first book on Nat Turner

1931   Rayford Logan portrays Nat Turner as a freedom fighter

1966   William Styron publishes *The Confessions of Nat Turner* and renews the controversy

While no one knows the way Nat Turner looked, this drawing by an unknown artist was used extensively during the nineteenth century to represent him in accounts of the uprising.

INTRODUCTION

Nat Turner: Man and Symbol

I learned about Nat Turner, as did many of my generation, in reverse chronological order, as you would if you were to read this book from back to front.

The history that I was taught, both in school and in college, was largely the story of heroic white men. Occasionally a George Washington Carver or an Eleanor Roosevelt popped in to play a minor role; but minorities and women seldom played the lead; and only those considered "positive" role models were permitted on the stage at all. Thus in all my history courses, even those that dealt with the United States before the Civil War, I was not introduced to Nat Turner.

The first time I became aware of his effect on the American Mind came during a heated confrontation between William Styron, the white novelist who had written a prize-winning fictional account of the Turner insurrection, and an angry black critic at a Southern Historical Association meeting in New Orleans in 1968. The face-off made me aware that a controversial work of fiction had escaped my attention for a year after its popular success and that an important historical figure had escaped my attention for the quarter century of my educational life. Intrigued by the controversy that the novel raised, with black critics condemning the white novelist for his racism, all of which epitomized the racial divisions of the sensitive 1960s, I not only read Styron's novel and the critiques of black respondents, but also took a fresh look at the history of slavery and slavery's lingering effects on American thought and life.

In the process I found the autobiographical works of Frederick Douglass and the accounts of others who escaped slavery. I found documents that presented the story of slavery and helped to explain its resultant racism; and among them was, of course, the story of Nat Turner, the revolt he led, and its effects on his own day as well as on subsequent American history. Oddly enough, I came even later to the original "confession" that Turner made to Thomas Gray just before his execution. You will find it much easier to read the story from 1831 to the present—from beginning to end, the right way— than to read it the way I did.

Here you will find a man, not white, not an elected official, not for the majority a "positive" role model, who nevertheless helped create the American Mind. You will meet Nat Turner, a man of his times, a slave in slave days, a real flesh-and-blood human being, with great strengths and great weaknesses like all of us, who through an extraordinary act, guided by an unusual vision, became more than just another man. He was a man who became a symbol of human courage reacting to oppression, an inspiration to the oppressed, a terror to the oppressor. As a symbol he continues to arouse interest and controversy well into the second century after his life and death. As a symbol he helps balance an American history often weighted against the people he tried to free. Both the man and the symbol helped create the American Mind.

NAT TURNER

Cry Freedom in America

PART I

Slavery:
The South's
"Peculiar Institution"

The slavery into which Nat Turner was born in 1800 was different from the slavery of earlier times in other parts of the world. Until the seventeenth century slaves were generally the losers in competition for economic gain or military superiority. They were often physically indistinguishable from their masters, they could with good fortune gain freedom, and their children did not have to remain in bondage. Only when Africans were brought to the Western Hemisphere was slavery identified exclusively with color and became in most cases a permanent condition. In the British colonies of North America and then in the independent United States of America skin color became the sole factor in determining who could be made and kept a slave, who was born into slavery and who was not.

It was not entirely clear, when the first Africans were brought to the British colonies in 1619, whether they would be kept slaves or freed upon completion of five to seven years of labor, as were white indentured servants. But quickly in those places where black slaves proved useful and profitable, laws were passed to keep them slaves—and their descendants automatically enslaved as well. Nat Turner was born in such a place under such laws. To slave parents he was born a slave, and he was to remain a slave all his life.

Slaves who felt the urge to rebel could follow one of three paths: they could passively resist their onerous work by feigning illness or incompetence or by sabotaging machinery; they could run away and hope they made it to free lands; or they could fight back, singly or collectively. Runaways who were caught and fighters risked severe punishment—and sometimes death. Yet there were many runaways, including probably Nat Turner's own father, and there were open rebellions, some involving large numbers of slaves. One such uprising was organized by Gabriel Prosser near Richmond, Virginia, in 1800; and one was organized by Denmark Vesey near Charleston, South Carolina, in 1822; but both uprisings were betrayed by other slaves, and both were suppressed by state militias. Yet Nat Turner's insurrection had a particularly strong impact on the nation, North and South. It was well organized by a charismatic leader, it was kept secret, it was at least momentarily successful, and it was bloody. Nat Turner became a symbol of rebellion against slavery, the prototypical slave who dared cry freedom in America, the slave who chose violent confrontation over passive acquiescence to bondage. He is as alive today as he was in 1831. He remains perhaps the most vibrant of all American slaves.

THE MEMORIES OF FREDERICK DOUGLASS

A young slave in Maryland, who was just fourteen years old when Nat Turner led his revolt, may or may not have known the details of the uprising in Virginia, but he probably knew that a rebellion had been attempted and had failed. When his time came, instead of organizing a revolt, he ran away. Nat Turner had inspired him to act, but his act was to flee. Seven years after Nat Turner died, Frederick Douglass ran away from his master, made his way to the North, and eventually purchased his freedom. He became a leader of the abolitionist cause, calling in his speeches, his books, and his editorials in his own newspaper for an end to slavery in the United States. In the following passage from his book *My Bondage and My Freedom* (originally published in 1845) he describes what it was like to be a slave and gives us clues as to why both he and Nat Turner would risk all for freedom:

My discontent grew upon me, and I was on the look-out for means of escape. With money, I could easily have managed the matter, and,

A portrait of Frederick Douglass as he appeared soon after his escape to freedom. His expression reveals both his fear of being enslaved again and his determination not to be.

therefore, I hit upon the plan of soliciting the privilege of hiring my time. It is quite common, in Baltimore, to allow slaves this privilege, and it is the practice, also, in New Orleans. A slave who is considered trustworthy, can, by paying his master a definite sum regularly, at the end of each week, dispose of his time as he likes. It so happened that I was not in very good odor, and I was far from being a trustworthy slave. Nevertheless, I watched my opportunity when Master Thomas came to Baltimore (for I was still his property, Hugh only acted as his agent) in the spring of 1838, to purchase his spring supply of goods, and applied to him, directly, for the much-coveted privilege of hiring my time. This request Master Thomas unhesitatingly refused to grant; and he charged me, with some sternness, with inventing this stratagem to make my escape. He told me, "I could *go nowhere* but he could catch me; and, in the event of my running away, I might be assured he should spare no pains in his efforts to recapture me. He recounted, with a good deal of eloquence, the many kind offices he had done me, and exhorted me to be contented and obedient. "Lay out no plans for the future," said he. "If you behave yourself properly, I will take care of you." Now, kind and considerate as this offer was, it failed to soothe me into repose. In spite of Master Thomas, and, I may say, in spite of myself, also, I continued to think, and worse still, to think almost exclusively about the injustice and wickedness of slavery. No effort of mine or of his could silence this trouble-giving thought, or change my purpose to run away.

About two months after applying to Master Thomas for the privilege of hiring my time, I applied to Master Hugh for the same liberty, supposing him to be unacquainted with the fact that I had made a similar application to Master Thomas, and had been refused. My boldness in making this request, fairly astounded him at the first. He gazed at me in amazement. But I had many good reasons for pressing the matter; and, after listening to them awhile, he did not absolutely refuse, but told me he would think of it. Here, then, was a gleam of hope. Once master of my own time, I felt sure that I could make, over and above my obligation to him, a dollar or two every week. Some slaves have made enough, in this way, to purchase their freedom. It is a sharp spur to industry; and some of the most enterprising colored men in Baltimore hire themselves in this way. After mature reflection—as I must suppose it was—Master Hugh granted me the privilege in question, on the following terms: I was to be allowed all my time; to make all bargains for work; to find my own employment, and to collect my own wages; and, in return for this liberty, I was required, or obliged, to pay him three dollars at the end of each week, and to board and clothe myself, and buy my own calking tools. A failure in any of these particulars would put an end to my privilege. This was a hard bargain. The wear and tear of clothing, the losing and breaking of tools, and the expense of board, made it necessary for me to earn at least six dollars per week, to keep even with the world. All who are acquainted with calking, know how uncertain and irregular that employment is. It can be done to advantage only in dry weather, for it is useless to put wet oakum into a seam. Rain or shine, however, work or no work, at the end of each week the money must be forthcoming.

Master Hugh seemed to be very much pleased, for a time, with this arrangement; and well he might be, for it was decidedly in his favor. It relieved him of all anxiety concerning me. His money was sure. He had armed my love of liberty with a lash and a driver, far more efficient than any I had before known; and, while he derived all the benefits of slaveholding by the arrangement, without its evils, I endured all the evils of being a slave, and yet suffered all the care and anxiety of a responsible freeman. "Nevertheless," thought I, "it is a valuable privilege—another step in my career toward freedom." It was something even to be permitted to stagger under the disadvantages of liberty, and I was determined to hold on to the newly gained footing, by all proper industry. I was ready to work by night as well as by day; and being in the enjoyment of excellent health, I was able not only to meet my current expenses, but also to lay by a small sum at the end of each week. All went on thus, from the month of May till August; then—for reasons which will become apparent as I proceed—my much valued liberty was wrested from me.

During the week previous to this (to me) calamitous event, I had made arrangements with a few young friends, to accompany them, on Saturday night, to a camp-meeting, held about twelve miles from Baltimore. On the evening of our intended start for the camp-ground, something occurred in the ship yard where I was at work, which detained me unusually late, and compelled me either to disappoint my young friends, or to neglect carrying my weekly dues to Master Hugh. Knowing that I had the money, and could hand it to him on another day, I decided to go to camp-meeting, and to pay him the three dollars, for the past week, on my return. Once on the camp-ground, I was induced to remain one day longer than I had intended, when I left home. But, as soon as I returned, I went straight to his house on Fell street, to hand him his (my) money. Unhappily, the fatal mistake had been committed. I found him exceedingly angry. He exhibited all the signs of apprehension and wrath, which a slaveholder may be surmised to exhibit on the supposed escape of a favorite slave. "You rascal! I have a great mind to give you a severe whipping. How dare you go out of the city without first asking and obtaining my permission?" "Sir," said I, "I hired my time and paid you the price you asked for it. I did not know that it was any part of the bargain that I should ask you when or where I should go."

"You did not know, you rascal! You are bound to show yourself here every Saturday night." After reflecting, a few moments, he became somewhat cooled down; but, evidently greatly troubled, he said, "Now, you scoundrel! you have done for yourself; you shall hire your time no longer. The next thing I shall hear of, will be your running away. Bring home your tools and your clothes, at once. I'll teach you how to go off in this way."

Thus ended my partial freedom. I could hire my time no longer; and I obeyed my master's orders at once. The little taste of liberty which I had had—although as the reader will have seen, it was far from being unalloyed—by no means enhanced my contentment with slavery. Punished thus by Master Hugh, it was now my turn to punish him. "Since," thought I, "you will make a slave of me, I will await your orders in all things," and, instead of going to look for work on Monday morning, as I had formerly done, I remained at home during the entire week, without the performance of a single stroke of work. Saturday night came, and he called upon me, as usual, for my wages. I, of course, told him I had done no work, and had no wages. Here we were at the point of coming to blows. His wrath had been accumulating during the whole week; for he evidently saw that I was making no effort to get work, but was most aggravatingly awaiting his orders, in all things. As I look back to this behavior of mine, I scarcely know what possessed me, thus to trifle with those who had such unlimited power to bless or to blast me. Master Hugh raved and swore his determination to "*get hold of me*," but, wisely for him, and happily for me, his wrath only employed those very harmless, impalpable missiles, which roll from a limber tongue. In my desperation, I had fully made up my mind to measure strength with Master Hugh, in case he should undertake to execute his threats. I am glad there was no necessity for this; for resistance to him could not have ended so happily for me, as it did in the case of Covey. He was not a man to be safely resisted by a slave; and I freely own, that in my conduct toward him, in this instance, there was more folly than wisdom. Master Hugh closed his reproofs, by telling me that, hereafter, I need give myself no uneasiness about getting work; that he "would, himself, see to getting work for me, and enough of it, at that." This threat I confess had some terror in it; and, on thinking the matter over, during the Sunday, I resolved, not only to save him the trouble of getting me work, but that, upon the third day of September, I would attempt to make my escape from slavery. The refusal to allow me to hire my time, therefore, hastened the period of flight. I had three weeks, now, in which to prepare for my journey.

Once resolved, I felt a certain degree of repose, and on Monday, instead of waiting for Master Hugh to seek employment for me, I was up by break of day, and off to the ship yard of Mr. Butler, on the City Block, near the draw-bridge. I was a favorite with Mr. B., and, young as I was, I had served as his foreman on the float stage, at calking. Of course, I easily obtained work, and, at the end of the week—which by the way was exceedingly fine—I brought Master Hugh nearly nine dollars. The effect of this mark of returning good sense, on my part, was excellent. He was very much pleased; he took the money, commended me, and told me I might have done the same thing the week before. It is a blessed thing that the tyrant may not always know the thoughts and purposes of his victim. Master Hugh little knew what my plans were. The going to camp-meeting without asking his permission—the insolent answers made to his reproaches—the sulky deportment the week after being deprived of the privilege of hiring my time—had awakened in him the suspicion that I might be cherishing disloyal purposes. My object, therefore, in working steadily, was to remove suspicion, and in this I succeeded admirably. He probably thought I was never better satisfied with my condition, than at the very time I was planning my escape. The second week passed, and again I carried him my full week's wages—nine *dollars*; and so well pleased was he, that he gave me TWENTY-FIVE CENTS! and "bade me make good use of it!" I told him I would, for one of the uses to which I meant to put it, was to pay my fare on the underground railroad.

Things without went on as usual; but I was passing through the same internal excitement and anxiety which I had experienced two years and a half before. The failure, in that instance, was not calculated to increase my confidence in the success of this, my second attempt; and I knew that a second failure could not leave me where my first did—I must either get to the *far north,* or be sent to the *far south.* Besides the exercise of mind from this state of facts, I had the painful sensation of being about to separate from a circle of honest and warm hearted friends, in Baltimore. The thought of such a separation, where the hope of ever meeting again is excluded, and where there can be no correspondence, is very painful. It is my opinion, that thousands would escape from slavery who now remain there, but for the strong cords of affection that bind them to their families, relatives and friends. The daughter is hindered from escaping, by the love she bears her mother, and the father, by the love he bears his children; and so, to the end of the chapter. I had no relations in Baltimore, and I saw no probability of ever living in the neighborhood of sisters and brothers; but the thought of leaving my friends, was among the strongest obstacles to my running away. The last two days of the week—Friday and Saturday—were spent mostly in collecting my things together, for my journey. Having worked four days that week, for my master, I handed him six dollars, on Saturday night. I seldom spent my Sundays at home, and, for fear that something might be discovered in my conduct, I kept up my custom, and absented myself all day. On Monday, the third day of September, 1838, in accordance with my resolution, I bade farewell to the city of Baltimore, and to that slavery which had been my abhorrence from childhood.

How I got away—in what direction I traveled—whether by land or by waters; whether with or without assistance—must, for reasons already mentioned, remain unexplained.

THE LIFE OF THE SLAVE NAT TURNER, AS TOLD BY STEPHEN OATES

But what of Nat Turner's life in slavery? To understand his rebellion, we must know the life he lived before setting out on his road of no return. Although slavery may have been in some ways the same for all slaves—restrictive, demeaning, exhausting—each slave faced and reacted to a different set of experiences. In the following excerpts from his excellent book on Nat Turner, *Fires of Jubilee*, respected historian Stephen Oates shows how the particular experience of Nat Turner the slave helped mold the character of Nat Turner the rebel. Nat has just been sent to a new plantation:

And so began a dispiriting new season of Nat's life. He now rose before first light, ate a breakfast of cornpone and mush, milked the cows and fed the hogs and chickens. Then at daybreak there came the haunting bellow of a horn, ordering him and the other hands to the fields, to work there until dusk. They spent March and April planting cotton. In the summer, as the plant sprouted in Southampton's lackluster soil, as gray as gunpowder, the slaves hoed and grubbed in the fields, battling squadrons of mosquitoes and gnats as they moved. All about them were the swampy forests, moving against a background of thunderheads. The woods seemed to wall in the meadows and fields, giving them an air of solitude and remoteness from all the world beyond.

At high sun Nat and the other hands stopped for dinner: a bite of meal, maybe some bacon fat or salt pork, brought with them from the cabins. For a while they would nap or talk and sing together. Then

Master Samuel or some hired driver would prod them, "Tumble up! Tumble up! Back to work with you." And so they passed the afternoons and evenings as they had the mornings. They picked worms off the cotton plants and then sowed corn and some tobacco in contiguous fields. Then they hoed these, too, singing all the while those spirituals that helped them endure their unendurable lives. They sang to their hoes, to the cotton leaves, the plows, the mules and oxen. And they sang in the quiet dust of the evening, on the way back to their unowned, shipwreck homes. They sang about the sorrow and sadness—the hopes and aspirations—of their lives under the lash: they sang about Moses warring in evil lands, about God smiting sinners and commanding them, "Let my people go." They sang of broken families, of whippings, of revenge against the white man. And they sang of better times ahead, when all would be gladness in the kingdom.

> No more rain fall for to wet you, Hallelujah,
> No more sun shine for to burn you,
> Dere's no whips a crackin'
> No evil-doers in de kingdom
> All is gladness in de kingdom.

So young Nat toiled through the days, observing all, forgetting nothing, as he wielded his clumsy hoe. In August the slaves stripped the tobacco leaves from the stalks and bundled them to dry. When a thunderstorm lashed the countryside, they labored in the shacks and sheds, fixing broken tools, helping the women or the skilled slaves. In September or October, the cotton leaves ripened and fell away from the bolls, transforming the fields into oceans of white. Now it was picking time—the blacks moving like slow freighters through a cotton sea. They picked until their shoulders and fingers ached to the bones, for they must gather the bolls before the frosts came. When that was done, they had to harvest the corn, too, and pull and stack the hay. In between planting and harvesting the crops, they repaired fences, cleared new fields, chopped firewood, and did a variety of other chores. Then in the spring the cycle started again, a monotonous, mind-killing cycle that measured the tick-tock passing of their lives. And so "the human cattle" moved, recalled Frederick Douglass, a former slave, "hurried on by no hope of reward, no sense of gratitude . . . no prospect of bettering their condition; nothing, save the dread and terror of the slave-driver's lash. So goes one day, and so comes and goes another."

* * *

As it went on farms and plantations across Virginia and the Carolinas, so it went on Samuel Turner's farm in tidewater Southampton County. Here, too, the slaves found in family life and holidays a marginal way to enjoy themselves, take the edge off despair, salvage traditional folk customs. Young Nat, however, rarely participated in their leisure-time amusements—and never in the drinking. A brooding, introspective youth, he preferred to spend his spare time either in prayer or in improving his knowledge. He experimented in making gunpowder and exploited every opportunity to read books. When Master Samuel hired a tutor to instruct his children, Nat found ways to look at their histories and geographies. And he discovered in those books, he claimed, many things "that the fertility of my own imagination had depicted to me before."

Still, it was religion that occupied Nat the most. At Negro praise meetings, he listened transfixed as black exhorters preached a different version of Christianity from what the white man offered, an alternate version that condemned slavery and fueled resistance to it. This was black religion—an amalgam of African mythology and Christian doctrines as slaves interpreted them, a unique religion that embodied the essence of the slaves' lives—their frustrations and sorrows, their memories, and their fantasies about a future world without whips and masters. An inquisitive youth, "observant of everything that was passing," Nat was quick to discern the power of the black preacher, who delivered his Bible sermons with stabbing gestures, singing out in rhythmic language that was charged with emotion and vivid imagery. He was an acknowledged leader—a sacred leader—who through his trembling expression, his cadences, inflections, and body movements articulated the deepest needs and feelings of his congregation. And the slaves, swept along by his magic, hummed and swayed in constant motion, punctuating his exhortation with "Amen" and "Hallelujah," with "Tell it to them, preacher." And then all joined in a moving spiritual, "O my Lord delivered Daniel," clapping, clapping, "O why not deliver me." Until the power of the music, the clapping and shouting, drove old and young alike into "a frenzy of religious fervor."

There can be no doubt that the slave church (now a forest clearing, now a tumbledown shack) nourished young Nat's self-esteem and his longing for independence. For the slave church was not only a center for underground slave plottings against the master class, but the focal point for an entire subterranean culture the blacks sought to construct beyond the white man's control. The church was both opiate and inspiration, a place where the slaves, through their ring-shout responses and their powerful and unique spirituals, could both escape their lot and protest against it. Here they could find comfort and courage in a black man's God, an animated Spirit, a *presence* who was with them every moment of their lives. Yes, the church was a place to "get happy," one slave recalled. A place where blacks could be "free indeed, free from death, free from hell, free from work, free from white folks, free from everything."

At one praise meeting, Nat was struck by a certain passage the preacher quoted from the Bible. "Seek ye the kingdom of Heaven," the preacher exclaimed, "and all things shall be added unto you." Afterward, Nat brooded over that passage. What did it mean? How did it apply to him? For weeks he prayed for light on the subject; and one day while praying at his plow Nat thought he heard a voice in the wind. It *was* a voice, he was certain of it, and as he stood rooted to the spot, he heard the Spirit call out to him as to the prophets of old, repeating the same scriptural passage the preacher had cited. Well, Nat was entranced, but he said nothing about his revelation to the other slaves, instead keeping more and more to himself and praying continuously. Then he heard it again, a wind-voice in the windswept trees: "Seek ye the kingdom of Heaven and all things shall be added unto you." At last it seemed clear to him. Because of his extraordinary qualities, Nat had been "ordained for some great purpose in the hands of the Almighty," a divine purpose that would one day be revealed to him. And he rejoiced in his communion with the Spirit and his closeness to the kingdom. And in the months and seasons that followed, he studied the Bible intensely, memorizing the books of the Old Testament, and grew to manhood with the words of the prophets roaring in his ears.

* * *

In 1819 a severe depression rocked the United States, and agricultural prices began an appalling downward spiral that was to last four years. The price of cotton, for example, fell from 30 cents a pound in the boom years to less than 10 cents a pound in 1823. Virginia was especially hard hit, so that farmers and planters alike were obliged to retrench and sell their excess slaves off to the Deep South. The Panic hurt Samuel Turner, too, but he balked at selling his Negroes. Instead he hired an overseer to get more work out of them and to manage the estate more efficiently.

Evidently the overseer arrived late in 1821. It seems clear that he flogged Nat, for shortly after he came the young exhorter ran away from him. Yes, he became a fugitive, driven into Southampton's swamps by some unrecorded cruelty and private anguish. ("O, why was I born a man, of whom to make a brute!" Frederick Douglass cried when he, too, decided to run. "I am left in the hottest hell of unending slavery. O, God, save me! God deliver me! Let me be free! is there any God? Why am I a slave? I will run away. I will not stand it. Get caught, or get clear, I'll try it. I have only one life to lose. I had as well be killed running as die standing.")

So Nat was gone, a slave patrol undoubtedly on his trail somewhere. And the Negroes back on Turner's farm prayed for him, recalling how Nat's father had escaped to freedom. Maybe Nat would make it, too.

But thirty days later Nat returned—walked right up to the Turner house, not in the custody of the slave patrol and a pack of hounds, but of his own free will. The other slaves were astonished. No fugitive ever came back on his own. "And the negroes found fault, and murmured against me," Nat confessed later, "saying that if they had my sense they would not serve any master in the world." Nat's reply? "The Spirit appeared to me and said I had my wishes directed to the things of this world, and not to the kingdom of heaven, and that I should return to the service of my earthly master." Nat said the same to Master Samuel, who was glad to have his property back, even if he must be punished. Then with exquisite irony Nat quoted the very Biblical passage white masters liked to foist on slaves: "For he who knoweth his Master's will, and doeth it not, shall be beaten with many stripes, and thus have I chastened you."

Oates goes on to explain that perhaps one reason why Nat returned was because he had fallen in love with a slave woman named Cherry, with whom he eventually had children. In 1822, however, Nat's life changed dramatically when his master died, leaving no mature heirs, and most of the slaves were sold. At first fearing that he would be sold to the Deep South, Nat was relieved to find that he had been purchased by Thomas Moore of Southampton County, that he would not be moving far, and that Cherry would be at a plantation close enough for him to visit, if at irregular times. He would occasionally see her and his children, but on the Moore plantation he would sleep alone. Oates continues:

Nat's new master was not a harsh man, but he clearly expected Nat to do heavy work or he would never have shelled out $400 for him. In fact, as an "expectant planter," a farmer on the rise, Moore worked his three field hands as hard as he drove himself in a grinding effort to raise profitable crops. By 1824, Moore's labors seemed worth the effort: farm prices stabilized in Virginia and even began to rise, and the long, racking depression seemed at an end.

And so Nat's days degenerated into endless, backbreaking drudgery. A sort of "all-purpose chattel," as one writer has described him, Nat built the morning fires, hauled water, fed the cows, slopped the hogs, chopped wood, raised fences, repaired fences, cleared new fields, spread manure, and grew and gathered hay for the stock. In the spring, he struggled through the damp fields behind a mule-drawn plow. Most of the summer he chopped and cut and hoed in the corn and cotton patches, battling weeds, weevils, and the weather itself. Then he had to harvest the crops before winter set in, wrestling with gunnysacks of cotton, corn, and apples, which Moore loaded in his wagon and took off to sell in Jerusalem on market Saturdays.

The work never seemed to let up; it was worse than anything Nat had known back on Samuel Turner's farm. And if Nat had felt betrayed there by false hopes, he must now have been beside himself with anguish. For even after his enigmatic runaway attempt, Nat had evidently retained some vague hope that one day he might be freed. Yes, freedom. Nat understood the meaning of that word only too well. Given his prodigious knowledge of the Bible and his intelligence ("He had a mind capable of attaining anything," a white man said), it was as inevitable as time itself that Nat should crave his freedom, dream of it, fantasize about it, even when it seemed increasingly dim and distant. As another slave, Lunsford Lane, recalled: "I saw no prospect that my condition would ever be changed. Yet I used to plan in my mind from day to day, and from night to night, how I might be free." Had Nat never been born on Benjamin Turner's place, had he never learned to read the Bible and other books, had he been whipped and beaten into mindless oblivion, then maybe he would not have despised his condition so. For it was as the preacher said in the Scriptures, "Knowledge increaseth sorrow." And here at Moore's farm Nat's sorrow was mounting daily: he was twenty-three years old, separated from his wife, caught in a maelstrom of mundane chores, the property of an ambitious young white man who was not about to unleash a $400 investment, so that freedom—so close in Nat's mind—was in reality more remote than ever.

Was *this* to be his destiny then? To spend the rest of his years behind a shitting mule in Moore's cotton patches? This could not be his purpose. There was more to his life than this. God did not intend a man of *his* gifts, *his* intelligence, *his* powers, to waste his years hoeing weeds and slopping hogs. To see his wife—poor enslaved sparrow—ordered and shoved around over at Reese's place, a victim of white people's every caprice, every whim. To toil and die like livestock (however affectionately treated) in this hypocritical Christian neighborhood, where white people gloried in the teachings of Jesus and yet discriminated against the "free coloreds" and kept all the other blacks in chains. Where slavemasters bragged about their benevolence ("In Virginia we take care of our 'niggers' ") and yet broke up families, sold Negroes off to whip-happy slave traders when money was scarce, and denied proud, godly men like Nat Turner something even the most debauched and useless poor whites enjoyed: their freedom.

QUESTIONS FOR RESPONSIVE ESSAYS

1. Historians have long debated the reason why slavery survived and flourished in the United States, even when the nation was built on the idea that all men are created equal. Some have said that people of African descent were kept slaves because the South's agricultural economy demanded a cheap labor force, whereas others have argued that a racism that predated the arrival of Africans in North America made possible the continued bondage of people of color. Using the knowledge of slavery that you have learned here, explain each argument and then defend the one you favor.

2. What do you learn about slavery by reading Frederick Douglass' account of his experience in bondage? What does his reaction to that bondage tell you about Frederick Douglass the man? How do you think the example of Nat Turner may have made him choose the alternative to rebellion: running away alone to freedom in the North?

3. From the account of Nat Turner's life related by Stephen Oates, what elements of slave life do you think caused a person of Nat's sensitivity and temperament to lead a revolt? What happened between his escape and return and his later rebellion to cause such a change in his attitude? What clues to Nat's personality can be found in each reaction, the escape and the later insurrection?

PART II

The "Confession" of Nat Turner

It was in August 1831 that Nat Turner led his insurrection against the white slaveholders of Southampton County, Virginia. The uprising lasted for two days and resulted in the deaths of fifty-five whites and more than one hundred slaves, most of the slaves killed in reprisal for the rising. Nat Turner, a literate, skilled artisan, a Christian minister to his local slave community, became a legend—and a symbol of violent rejection of bondage.

Nat Turner was born a slave in 1800, but in childhood, due to natural talent and odd twists of fate, he was accorded unusual treatment. He became a house servant rather than a field hand, and he was permitted to learn reading and writing. Then his condition changed; and at age twenty-one, as we have seen, he ran away, only to return after a month for reasons largely unknown. At age twenty-five he received what he believed was a vision from God, and three years later came a second one. Both visions he took to mean that he was to lead his people in a great battle for freedom. He interpreted an eclipse of the sun on August 13, 1831, as a sign that it was time to act. Action for him meant, to begin with, killing white slave owners.

After the insurrection was ended by military force, Nat Turner hid for more than two months before he was captured and lodged

THE
CONFESSIONS

OF

NAT TURNER,

THE LEADER OF THE LATE

INSURRECTION IN SOUTHAMPTON, VA.

As fully and voluntarily made to

THOMAS R. GRAY,

In the prison where he was confined, and acknowledged by him to be such when read before the Court of South- ampton; with the certificate, under seal of the Court convened at Jerusalem, Nov. 5, 1831, for his trial.

ALSO, AN AUTHENTIC

ACCOUNT OF THE WHOLE INSURRECTION,

WITH LISTS OF THE WHITES WHO WERE MURDERED,

AND OF THE NEGROES BROUGHT BEFORE THE COURT OF SOUTHAMPTON, AND THERE SENTENCED, &c.

Baltimore:
PUBLISHED BY THOMAS R. GRAY.
Lucas & Deaver, print.
1831.

The cover page of the original "Confession" of Nat Turner to Thomas Gray, published in Baltimore in 1831. Controversy over the uprising caused sales to be brisk and prolonged.

in the Southampton County Jail in the town of Jerusalem, Virginia. In a one-day trial, at which his "confession" was read to the public, he was convicted and sentenced to death. Six days later he was hanged. From November 1 to November 3, 1831, just before he was tried and sentenced to death, Nat Turner dictated his "confession" to a white man named Thomas Gray. It is difficult to prove how much, if any, of the testimony is Gray's interpolation; but scholars tend to trust Gray's assertion that it was a faithful rendering of Nat's words and thoughts. It is Nat Turner's first, last, and only testament about who he was, what he did, and why he did it. The opening words are those of Thomas Gray, addressing the court, adding his commentary to the "confession" that follows:

The late insurrection in Southampton has greatly excited the public mind, and led to a thousand idle, exaggerated and mischievous reports. It is the first instance in our history of an open rebellion of the slaves, and attended with such atrocious circumstances of cruelty and destruction, as could not fail to leave a deep impression, not only upon the minds of the community where this fearful tragedy was wrought, but throughout every portion of our country, in which this population is to be found. Public curiosity has been on the stretch to understand the origin and progress of this dreadful conspiracy, and the motives which influence its diabolical actors. The insurgent slaves had all been destroyed, or apprehended, tried and executed (with the exception of the leader), without revealing any thing at all satisfactory, as to the motives which governed them, or the means by which they expected to accomplish their object. Every thing connected with the sad affair was wrapt in mystery, until Nat Turner, the leader of this ferocious band, whose name has resounded throughout our widely extended empire, was captured. This "great Bandit" was taken by a single individual, in a cave near the residence of his late owner, on Sunday, the thirtieth of October, without attempting to make the slightest resistance, and on the following day safely lodged in the jail of the county. His captor was Benjamin Phipps, armed with a shot gun well charged. Nat's only weapon was a small light sword which he immediately surrendered, and begged that his life might be spared. Since his confinement, by permission of the Jailor, I have had ready access to him, and finding that he was willing to make a full and free confession of the origin, progress and consummation of the insurrectory movements of the slaves of which he was the contriver and head; I determined for the gratification of public curiosity to commit his statements to writing, and publish them, with little or no variation, from his own words. That this is a faithful record of his confessions, the annexed certificate of the County Court of Southampton, will attest. They certainly bear one stamp of truth and sincerity. He makes no attempt (as all the other insurgents who were examined did) to exculpate himself, but frankly acknowledges his full participation in all the guilt of the transaction. He was not only the contriver of the conspiracy, but gave the first blow towards its execution.

It will thus appear, that whilst every thing upon the surface of society wore a calm and peaceful aspect; whilst not one note of preparation was heard to warn the devoted inhabitants of woe and death, a gloomy fanatic was revolving in the recesses of his own dark, bewildered, and overwrought mind, schemes of indiscriminate massacre to the whites. Schemes too fearfully executed as far as his fiendish band proceeded in their desolating march. No cry for mercy penetrated their flinty bosoms. No acts of remembered kindness made the least impression upon these remorseless murderers. Men, women and children, from hoary age to helpless infancy were involved in the same cruel fate. Never did a band of savages do their work of death more unsparingly. Apprehension for their own personal safety seems to have been the only principle of restraint in the whole course of their bloody proceedings. And it is not the least remarkable feature in this horrid transaction, that a band actuated by such hellish purposes, should have resisted so feebly, when met by the whites in arms. Desperation alone, one would think, might have led to greater efforts. More than twenty of them attacked Dr. Blunt's house on Tuesday morning, a little before daybreak, defended by two men and three boys. They fled precipitately at the first fire; and their future plans of mischief, were entirely disconcerted and broken up. Escaping thence, each individual sought his own safety either in concealment, or by returning home, with the hope that his participation might escape detection, and all were shot down in the course of a few days, or captured and brought to trial and punishment. Nat has survived all his followers, and the gallows will speedily close his career. His own account of the conspiracy is submitted to the public, without comment. It reads an awful, and it is hoped, a useful lesson, as to the operations of a mind like his, endeavoring to grapple with things beyond its reach. How it first became bewildered and confounded and perpetration of the most atrocious and heart-rending deeds. It is calculated also to demonstrate the policy of our laws in restraint of this class of our population, and to induce all those entrusted with their execution, as well as our citizens generally, to see that they are strictly and rigidly enforced. Each particular community should look to its own safety, whilst the general guardians of the laws, keep a watchful eye over all. If Nat's statements can be relied on, the insurrection in this county was entirely local, and his designs confided but to a few, and these in his immediate vicinity. It was not instigated by motives of revenge or sudden anger, but the results of long deliberation, and a settled purpose of mind. The offspring of gloomy fanaticism, acting upon materials but too well prepared for such impressions. It will be long remembered in the annals of our country, and many a mother as she presses her infant darling to her bosom, will shudder at the recollection of Nat Turner, and his band of ferocious miscreants.

Believing the following narrative, by removing doubts and conjectures from the public mind which otherwise must have remained, would give general satisfaction, it is respectfully submitted to the public by their ob't serv't,

T. R. GRAY

Jerusalem, Southampton, Va. Nov. 5, 1831.

We the undersigned, members of the Court convened at Jerusalem, on Saturday, the 5th day of Nov. 1831, for the trial of Nat, *alias* Nat Turner, a negro slave, late the property of Putnam Moore, deceased, do hereby certify, that the confessions of Nat, to Thomas R. Gray, was read to him in our presence, and that Nat acknowledged the same to be full, free, and voluntary; and that furthermore, when called upon by the presiding Magistrate of the Court, to state if he had any thing to say, why sentence of death should not be passed upon him, replied he had nothing further than he had communicated to Mr. Gray. Given under our hands and seals at Jerusalem, this 5th day of November, 1831.

JEREMIAH COBB
THOMAS PRETLOW
JAMES W. PARKER
CARR BOWERS
SAMUEL B. HINES
ORRIS A. BROWNE

State of Virginia, Southampton County, to wit:

I, James Rochelle, Clerk of the County Court of Southampton in the State of Virginia, do hereby certify, that Jeremiah Cobb, Thomas Pretlow, James W. Parker, Carr Bowers, Samuel B. Hines, and Orris A.

Browne, esqr's are acting Justices of the Peace, in and for the County aforesaid, and were members of the Court which convened at Jerusalem, on Saturday the 5th day of November, 1831, for the trial of Nat *alias* Nat Turner, a negro slave, late the property of Putnam Moore, deceased, who was tried and convicted, as an insurgent in the late insurrection in the county of Southampton aforesaid, and that full faith and credit are due, and ought to be given to their acts as Justices of the peace aforesaid.

In testimony whereof, I have hereunto set my hand and caused the seal of the Court aforesaid, to be affixed this 5th day of November, 1831

JAMES ROCHELLE,

C. S. C. C.

SIR,—You have asked me to give a history of the motives which induced me to undertake the late insurrection as you call it—To do so I must go back to the days of my infancy, and even before I was born. I was thirty-one years of age the 2d of October last, and born the property of Benj. Turner, of this county. In my childhood a circumstance occurred which made an indelible impression on my mind, and laid the ground work of that enthusiasm, which has terminated so fatally to many, both white and black, and for which I am about to atone at the gallows. It is here necessary to relate this circumstance—trifling as it may seem, it was the commencement of that belief which has grown with time, and even now, sir, in this dungeon, helpless and forsaken as I am, I cannot divest myself of. Being at play with other children, when three or four years old, I was telling them something, which my mother overhearing, said it had happened before I was born—I stuck to my story, however, and related somethings which went, in her opinion, to confirm it—others being called on were greatly astonished, knowing that these things had happened, and caused them to say in my hearing, I surely would be a prophet, as the Lord had shewn me things that had happened before my birth. And my father and mother strengthened me in this my first impression, saying in my presence, I was intended for some great purpose, which they had always thought from certain marks on my head and breast—[a parcel of excrescences which I believe are not at all uncommon, particularly among negroes, as I have seen several with the same. In this case he has either cut them off or they have nearly disappeared]—My grandmother, who was very religious, and to whom I was much attached—my master, who belonged to the church, and other religious persons who visited the house, and whom I often saw at prayers, noticing the singularity of my manners, I suppose, and my uncommon intelligence for a child, remarked I had too much sense to be raised, and if I was, I would never be of any service to any one as a slave—To a mind like mine, restless, inquisitive and observant of every thing that was passing, it is easy to suppose that religion was the subject to which it would be directed, and although this subject principally occupied my thoughts—there was nothing that I saw or heard of to which my attention was not directed—The manner in which I learned to read and write, not only had great influence on my own mind, as I acquired it with the most perfect ease, so much so, that I have no recollection whatever of learning the alphabet—but to the astonishment of the family, one day, when a book was shewn me to keep me from crying, I began spelling the names of different objects—this was a source of wonder to all in the neighborhood, particularly the blacks—and this learning was constantly improved at all opportunities—when I got large enough to go to work, while employed, I was reflecting on many things that would present themselves to my imagination, and whenever an opportunity occurred of looking at a book, when the school children were getting their lessons, I would find many things that the fertility of my own imagination had depicted to me before; all my time, not devoted to my master's service, was spent either in prayer, or in making experiments in casting different things in moulds made of earth, in attempting to make paper, gun-powder, and many other experiments, that although I could not perfect, yet convinced me of its practicability if I had the means.[1] I was not addicted to stealing in my youth, nor have ever been—Yet such was the confidence of the negroes in the neighborhood, even at this early period of my life, in my superior judgment, that they would often carry me with them when they were going on any roguery, to plan for them. Growing up among them, with this confidence in my superior judgment, and when this, in their opinions, was perfected by Divine inspiration, from the circumstances already alluded to in my infancy, and which belief was ever afterwards zealously inculcated by the austerity of my life and manners, which became the subject of remark by white and black.—Having soon discovered to be great, I must appear so, and therefore studiously avoided mixing in society, and wrapped myself in mystery, devoting my time to fasting and prayer—By this time, having arrived to man's estate, and hearing the scriptures commented on

---

[1] When questioned as to the manner of manufacturing those different articles, he was found well informed on the subject.

at meetings, I was struck with that particular passage which says: "Seek ye the kingdom of Heaven and all things shall be added unto you." I reflected much on this passage, and prayed daily for light on this subject—As I was praying one day at my plough, the spirit spoke to me, saying "Seek ye the kingdom of heaven and all things shall be added unto you."

QUESTION: what do you mean by the Spirit. ANSWER: The Spirit that spoke to the prophets in former days—and I was greatly astonished, and for two years prayed continually, whenever my duty would permit—and then again I had the same revelation, which fully confirmed me in the impression that I was ordained for some great purpose in the hands of the Almighty.

Several years rolled round, in which many events occurred to strengthen me in this my belief. At this time I reverted in my mind to the remarks made of me in my childhood, and the things that had been shown me—and as it had been said of me in my childhood by those by whom I had been taught to pray, both white and black, and in whom I had the greatest confidence, that I had too much sense to be raised, and if I was, I would never be of any use to any one as a slave. Now finding I had arrived to man's estate, and was a slave, and these revelations being made known to me, I began to direct my attention to this great object, to fulfil the purpose for which, by this time, I felt assured I was intended. Knowing the influence I had obtained over the minds of my fellow servants, (not by the means of conjuring and such like tricks—for to them I always spoke of such things with contempt) but by the communions of the Spirit whose revelations I often communicated to them, and they believed and said my wisdom came from God. I now began to prepare them for my purpose, by telling them something was about to happen that would terminate in fulfilling the great promise that had been made to me— About this time I was placed under an overseer, from whom I ran away—and after remaining in the woods thirty days, I returned, to the astonishment of the Negroes on the plantation, who thought I had made my escape to some other part of the country, as my father had done before. But the reason of my return was, that the Spirit appeared to me and said I had my wishes directed to the things of this world, and not to the kingdom of Heaven, and that I should return to the service of my earthly master—"For he who knoweth his Master's will, and doeth it not, shall be beaten with many stripes, and thus have I chastened you." And the negroes found fault, and murmured against me saying that if they had my sense they would not serve any master in the world. And about this time I had a vision—and I saw white spirits and black spirits engaged in battle, and the sun was darkened—the thunder rolled in the Heavens, and blood flowed in streams—and I heard a voice saying, "Such is your luck, such you are called to see, and let it come rough or smooth, you must surely bare it." I now withdrew myself as much as my situation would permit, from the intercourse of my fellow servants, for the avowed purpose of serving the Spirit more fully—and it appeared to me, and reminded me of the things it had already shown me, and that it would then reveal to me the knowledge of the elements, the revolution of the planets, the operation of tides, and changes of the seasons. After this revelation in the year 1825, and the knowledge of the elements being made known to me, I sought more than ever to obtain true holiness before the great day of judgment should appear, and then I began to receive the true knowledge of faith. And from the first steps of righteousness until the last, was I made perfect; and the Holy Ghost was with me, and said, "Behold me as I stand in the Heavens"—and I looked and saw the forms of men in different attitudes—and there were lights in the sky to which the children of darkness gave other names than what they really were—for they were the lights of the Saviour's hands, stretched forth from east to west, even as they were extended on the cross on Calvary for the redemption of sinners. And I wondered greatly at these miracles, and prayed to be informed of a certainty of the meaning thereof—and shortly afterwards, while laboring in the field, I discovered drops of blood on the corn as though it were dew from heaven—and I communicated it to many, both white and black, in the neighborhood—and I then found on the leaves in the woods hieroglyphic characters, and numbers, with the forms of men in different attitudes, portrayed in blood, and representing the figures I had seen before in the heavens. And now the Holy Ghost had revealed itself to me, and made plain the miracles it had shown me—For as the blood of Christ had been shed on this earth, and had ascended to heaven for the salvation of sinners, and was now returning to earth again in the form of dew—and as the leaves on the trees bore the impression of the figures I had seen in the heavens, it was plain to me that the Saviour was about to lay down the yoke he had borne for the sins of men, and the great day of judgment was at hand. About this time I told these things to a white man, (Etheldred T. Brantley) on whom it had a wonderful effect—and he ceased from his wickedness, and was attacked immediately with a cutaneous eruption, and blood oozed from the pores of his skin, and after praying and fasting nine days, he was healed, and the Spirit appeared to me again, and said, as the Saviour had been baptised so should we be also—and when the white people would not let us be baptised by the church, we went down into the water together, in the sight of many who reviled us, and were baptised by the Spirit—After this I rejoiced greatly, and gave thanks to God. And on the 12th of May, 1828, I heard a loud noise in the heavens, and the Spirit instantly appeared to me and said the Serpent was loosened, and Christ had laid down the yoke he had borne for the sins of men, and that I should take it on and fight against the Serpent, for the time was fast approaching when the first should be last and the last should be first.

QUESTION: Do you not find yourself mistaken now? **ANSWER:**   Was not Christ crucified.

Nat Turner and his coconspirators continued to capture the imagination of artists throughout the nineteenth century. He is depicted here plotting strategy with his followers.

And by signs in the heavens that it would make known to me when I should commence the great work—and until the first sign appeared, I should conceal it from the knowledge of men—And on the appearance of the sign, (the eclipse of the sun last February) I should arise and prepare myself, and slay my enemies with their own weapons. And immediately on the sign appearing in the heavens, the seal was removed from my lips, and I communicated the great work laid out for me to do, to four in whom I had the greatest confidence (Henry, Hark, Nelson, and Sam)—it was intended by us to have begun the work of death on the 4th July last—Many were the plans formed and rejected by us, and it affected my mind to such a degree, that I fell sick, and the time passed without our coming to any determination how to commence—Still forming new schemes and rejecting them, when the sign appeared again, which determined me not to wait longer.

Since the commencement of 1830, I had been living with Mr. Joseph Travis, who was to me a kind master, and placed the greatest confidence in me; in fact, I had no cause to complain of his treatment to me. On Saturday evening, the 20th of August, it was agreed between Henry, Hark and myself, to prepare a dinner the next day for the men we expected, and then to concert a plan, as we had not yet determined on any. Hark, on the following morning, brought a pig, and Henry brandy, and being joined by Sam, Nelson, Will and Jack, they prepared in the woods a dinner, where, about three o'clock, I joined them.

QUESTION: Why were you so backward in joining them.

ANSWER: The same reason that had caused me not to mix with them for years before.

I saluted them on coming up, and asked Will how came he there, he answered, his life was worth no more than others, and his liberty as dear to him. I asked him if he thought to obtain it? He said he would or loose his life. This was enough to put him in full confidence. Jack, I knew, was only a tool in the hands of Hark, it was quickly agreed we should commence at home (Mr. J. Travis') on that night, and until we had armed and equipped ourselves, and gathered sufficient force, neither age nor sex was to be spared, (which was invariably adhered to). We remained at the feast, until about two hours in the night, when we went to the house and found Austin; they all went to the cider press and drank, except myself. On returning to the house, Hark went to the door with an axe, for the purpose of breaking it open, as we knew we were strong enough to murder the family, if they were

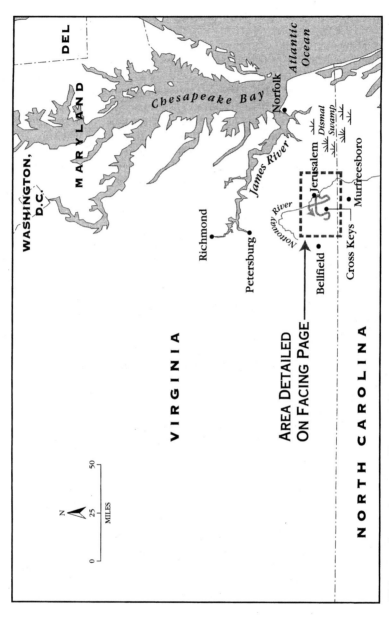

This map shows the area of Virginia where the Turner Rebellion occurred.

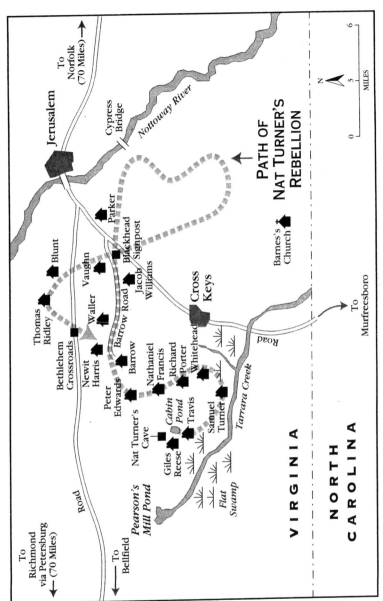

This map shows homes in the area touched directly by the Turner Rebellion.

33

awaked by the noise; but reflecting that it might create an alarm in the neighborhood, we determined to enter the house secretly, and murder them whilst sleeping. Hark got a ladder and set it against the chimney, on which I ascended, and hoisting a window, entered and came down stairs, unbarred the door, and removed the guns from their places. It was then observed that I must spill the first blood. On which, armed with a hatchet, and accompanied by Will, I entered my master's chamber, it being dark, I could not give a death blow, the hatchet glanced from his head, he sprang from the bed and called his wife, it was his last work, Will laid him dead, with a blow of his axe, and Mrs. Travis shared the same fate, as she lay in bed. The murder of this family, five in number was the work of a moment, not one of them awoke; there was a little infant sleeping in a cradle, that was forgotten, until we had left the house and gone some distance, when Henry and Will returned and killed it; we got here, four guns that

These two photographs by Henry Irving Tragle show 1) the Whitehead house where seven family members were killed; and 2) the spot where Nat turner found Margaret Whitehead hiding.

would shoot, and several old muskets, with a pound or two of powder. We remained some time at the barn, where we paraded; I formed them in a line as soldiers, and after carrying them through all the manoeuvres I was master of, marched them off to Mr. Salathul Francis', about six hundred yards distant. Sam and Will went to the door and knocked. Mr. Francis asked who was there, Sam replied it was him, and he had a letter for him, on which he got up and came to the door; they immediately seized him, and dragging him out a little from the door, he was dispatched by repeated blows on the head; there was no other white person in the family. We started from there for Mrs. Reese's, maintaining the most perfect silence on our march, where finding the door unlocked, we entered, and murdered Mrs. Reese in her bed, while sleeping; her son awoke, but it was only to sleep the sleep of death, he had only time to say who is that, and he was no more. From Mrs. Reese's we went to Mrs. Turner's, a mile distant, which we reached about sunrise, on Monday morning. Henry, Austin, and Sam, went to the still, where, finding Mr. Peebles, Austin shot him, and the rest of us went to the house; as we approached, the family discovered us, and shut the door. Vain hope! Will, with one stroke of his axe, opened it, and we entered and found Mrs. Turner and Mrs. Newsome in the middle of a room, almost frightened to death. Will immediately killed Mrs. Turner, with one blow of his axe. I took Mrs. Newsome by the hand, and with the sword I had when I was apprehended, I struck her several blows over the head, but not being able to kill her, as the sword was dull. Will turning around and discovering it, despatched her also. A general destruction of property and search for money and ammunition, always succeeded the murders. By this time my company amounted to fifteen, and nine men mounted, who started for Mrs. Whitehead's, (the other six were to go through a by way to Mr. Bryant's, and rejoin us at Mrs. Whitehead's), as we approached the house we discovered Mr. Richard Whitehead standing in the cotton patch, near the lane fence; we called him over into the lane, and Will, the executioner, was near at hand, with his fatal axe, to send him to an untimely grave. As we pushed on to the house, I discovered some one run round the garden, and thinking it was some of the white family, I pursued them, but finding it was a servant girl belonging to the house, I returned to commence the work of death, but they whom I left, had not been idle; all the family were already murdered, but Mrs. Whitehead and her daughter Margaret. As I came round to the door I saw Will pulling Mrs. Whitehead out of the house, and at the step he nearly severed her head from her body, with his broad axe. Miss Margaret, when I discovered her, had concealed herself in the corner, formed by the projection of the cellar cap from the house; on my approach she fled, but was soon overtaken, and after repeated blows with a sword, I killed her by a blow on the head, with a fence rail. By this time, the six who had gone by Mr. Bryant's, rejoined us, and informed me they had done the work of death assigned them. We again divided, part going to Mr. Richard Porter's, and from thence to Nathaniel Francis', the others to Mr. Howell Harris', and Mr. T. Doyle's. On my reaching Mr. Porter's, he had escaped with his family. I understood there, that the alarm had already spread, and I immediately returned to bring up those sent to Mr. Doyle's, and Mr. Howell Harris'; the party I left going on to Mr. Francis', having told them I would join them in that neighborhood. I met these sent to Mr. Doyle's and Mr. Harris' returning, having met Mr. Doyle on the road and killed him; and learning from some who joined them, that Mr. Harris was from home, I immediately pursued the course taken by the party gone on before; but knowing they would complete the work of death and pillage, at Mr. Francis' before I could get there, I went to Mr. Peter Edwards', expecting to find them there, but they had been here also. I then went to Mr. John T. Barrow's, they had been here and murdered him. I pursued on their track to Capt. Newit Harris', where I found the greater part mounted, and ready to start; the men now amounting to about forty, shouted and hurraed as I rode up, some were in the yard, loading their guns, others drinking. They said Captain Harris and his family had escaped, the property in the house they destroyed, robbing him of money and other valuables. I ordered them to mount and march instantly, this was about nine or ten o'clock, Monday morning. I proceeded to Mr. Levi Waller's, two or three miles distant, I took my station in the rear, and as it 'twas my object to carry terror and devastation wherever we went, I placed fifteen or twenty of the best armed and most to be relied on, in front, who generally approached the houses as fast as their horses could run; this was for two purposes, to prevent their escape and strike terror to the inhabitants—on this account I never got to the houses, after leaving Mrs. Whitehead's, until the murders were committed, except in one case. I sometimes got in sight in time to see the work of death completed, viewed the mangled bodies as they lay, in silent satisfaction, and immediately started in quest of other victims—Having murdered Mrs. Waller and ten children, we started for Mr. William Williams'—having killed him and two little boys that were there; while engaged in this, Mrs. Williams fled and got some distance from the house, but she was pursued, overtaken, and compelled to get up behind one of the company, who brought her back, and after showing her the mangled body of her lifeless husband, she was told to get down and lay by his side, where she was shot dead. I then started for Mr. Jacob Williams, where the family were murdered—Here we found a young man named Drury, who had come on business with Mr. Williams—he was pursued, overtaken and shot. Mrs. Vaughan was the next place we visited—and after murdering the family here, I determined on starting for Jerusalem—Our number amounted now to fifty or sixty, all mounted and armed with guns, axes, swords and clubs—On reaching Mr. James W. Parker's gate, immediately on the road leading to Jerusalem, and about three miles distant, it was proposed to me to call there, but I objected, as I knew he was gone to Jerusalem, and my object was to reach there as soon as possible; but some of the men having relations at Mr. Parker's it was agreed that they might call and get his people. I remained at the gate on the road, with seven or eight; the others going across the field to the house, about half a mile off. After waiting some time for them, I became impatient, and started to the house for them, and on our return we were met by a party of white men, who had pursued our blood-stained track, and who had fired on those at the gate, and dispersed them, which I knew nothing of, not having been at that time rejoined by any of them—Immediately on discovering the whites, I ordered my men to halt and form, as they appeared to be alarmed— The white men, eighteen in number, approached us in about one hundred yards, when one of them fired, (this was against the positive orders of Captain Alexander P. Peete, who commanded, and who had directed the men to reserve their fire until within thirty paces) And I discovered about half of them retreating, I then ordered my men to fire and rush on them; the few remaining stood their ground until we approached within fifty yards, when they fired and retreated. We pursued and overtook some of them who we thought we left dead; (they were not killed) after pursuing them about two hundred yards, and rising a little hill, I discovered they were met by another party, and had halted, and were re-loading their guns, (this was a small party from Jerusalem who knew the negroes were in the field, and had just tied their horses to await their return to the road, knowing that Mr. Parker and family were in Jerusalem, but knew nothing of the party that had gone in with Captain Peete; on hearing the firing they immediately rushed to the spot and arrived just in time to arrest the progress of these barbarious villains, and save the lives of their friends and fellow citizens.) Thinking that those who retreated first, and the party who fired on us at fifty or sixty yards distant, had all only fallen back to meet others with ammunition. As I saw them re-loading their guns, and more coming up than I saw at first, and several of my bravest men being wounded, the others became panick struck and squandered over the field; the white men pursued and fired on us several times. Hark had his horse shot under him, and I caught another for him as it was running by me; five or six of my men were wounded, but none left on the field; finding myself defeated here I instantly determined to go through a private way, and cross the Nottoway river at the Cypress Bridge, three miles below Jerusalem, and attack that place in the rear, as I expected they would look for me on the other road, and I had a great desire to get there to procure arms and ammunition. After going a short distance in this private way, accompanied by about twenty men, I overtook two or three who told me the others were dispersed in every direction. After trying in vain to collect a sufficient force to proceed to Jerusalem, I determined to return, as I was sure they would make back to their old neighborhood, where they would rejoin me, make new recruits, and come down again. On my way back, I called at Mrs. Thomas', Mrs. Spencer's, and several other places, the white families having fled, we found no more victims to gratify our thirst for blood, we stopped at Majr Ridley's quarter for the night, and being joined by four of his men, with the recruits made since my defeat, we mustered now about forty strong. After placing out sentinels, I laid down to sleep, but was quickly roused by a great racket; starting up, I found some mounted, and others in great confusion; one of the sentinels having given the alarm that we were about to be attacked, I ordered some to ride round and reconnoitre, and on their return the others being more alarmed, not knowing who they were, fled in different ways, so that I was reduced to about twenty again; with this I determined to attempt to recruit, and proceed on to rally in the neighborhood, I had left. Dr. Blunt's was the nearest house, which we reached just before day; on riding up the yard, Hark fired a gun. We expected Dr. Blunt and his family were at Maj. Ridley's, as I knew there was a company of men there; the gun was fired to ascertain if any of the family were at home; we were immediately fired upon and retreated, leaving several of my men. I do not know what became of them, as I never saw them afterwards. Pursuing our course back and coming in sight of Captain Harris', where we had been the day before, we discovered a party of white men at the house, on which all deserted me but two, (Jacob and Nat), we concealed ourselves in the woods until near night, when I sent them in search of Henry, Sam, Nelson, and Hark, and directed them to rally all they could, at the place we had had our dinner the Sunday before, where they would find me, and I accordingly returned there as soon as it was dark and remained until Wednesday evening, when discovering white men riding around the place as though they were looking for some one, and none of my men joining me, I concluded Jacob and Nat had been taken, and compelled to betray me. On this I gave up all hope for the present; and on Thursday night after having supplied myself with provisions from Mr. Travis', I scratched a hole under a pile of fence rails in a field, where I concealed myself for six weeks, never leaving my hiding place but for a few minutes in the dead of night to get water which was very near; thinking by this time I could venture out, I began to go about in the night and eaves drop the houses in the neighborhood; pursuing this course for about a fortnight and gathering little or no intelligence, afraid of speaking to any human being, and returning every morning to my cave before the dawn of day. I know not how long I might have led this life, if accident had not betrayed me, a dog in the neighborhood passing by my hiding place one night while I was out, was attracted by some meat I had in my cave, and crawled in and stole it, and was coming out just as I returned. A few nights after, two negroes having started to go hunting with the same dog, and passed that way, the dog came again to the place, and having just gone out to walk about, discovered me and barked, on which thinking myself discovered, I spoke to them to beg concealment. On making myself known they fled from me. Knowing then they would betray me, I immediately left my hiding place, and was pursued almost incessantly until I was taken a fortnight afterwards by Mr. Benjamin Phipps, in a little hole I had dug out with my sword, for the purpose of concealment, under the top of a fallen tree. On Mr. Phipps' discovering the place of my concealment, he cocked his gun and aimed at me. I requested him not to shoot and I would give up, upon which he demanded my sword. I delivered it to him, and he brought me to prison. During the time I was pursued, I had many hair breadth escapes, which your time will not permit you to relate. I am here loaded with chains, and willing to suffer the fate that awaits me.

With that, Nat Turner ends his statement, and Gray continues:

I here proceeded to make some inquiries of him, after assuring him of the certain death that awaited him, and that concealment would only bring destruction on the innocent as well as guilty, of his own color, if he knew of any extensive or concerted plan. His answer was, I do not. When I questioned him as to the insurrection in North Carolina happening about the same time, he denied any knowledge of it; and when I looked him in the face as though I would search his inmost thoughts, he replied, "I see sir, you doubt my word; but can you not think the same ideas, and strange appearances about this time in the heaven's might prompt others, as well as myself, to this undertaking." I now had much conversation with and asked him many questions, having forborne to do so previously, except in the cases noted in parenthesis; but during his statement, I had, unnoticed by him, taken notes as to some particular circumstances, and having the advantage of his statement before me in writing, on the evening of the third day that I had been with him, I began a cross examination, and found his statement corroborated by every circumstance coming within my own knowledge or the confessions of others whom had been either killed or executed, and whom he had not seen nor had any knowledge since 22d of August last, he expressed himself fully satisfied as to the impracticability of his attempt. It has been said he was ignorant and cowardly, and that his object was to murder and rob for the purpose of obtaining money to make his escape. It is notorious, that he was never known to have a dollar in his life; to swear an oath, or drink a drop of spirits. As to his ignorance, he certainly never had the advantages of education, but he can read and write, (it was taught him by his parents), and for natural intelligence and quickness of apprehension, is surpassed by few men I have ever seen. As to his being a coward, his reason as given for not resisting Mr. Phipps, shews the decision of his character. When he saw Mr. Phipps present his gun, he said he knew it was impossible for him to escape as the woods were full of men; he therefore thought it was better to surrender, and trust to fortune for his escape. He is a complete fanatic, or plays his part most admirably. On other subjects he possesses an uncommon share of intelligence, with a mind capable of attaining any thing; but warped and perverted by the influence of early impressions. He is below the ordinary stature, though strong and active, having the true negro face, every feature of which is strongly marked. I shall not attempt to describe the effect of his narrative, as told and commented on by himself, in the condemned hole of the prison. The calm, deliberate composure with which he spoke of his late deeds and intentions, the expression of his fiend-like face when excited by enthusiasm, still bearing the stains of the blood of helpless innocence about him; clothed with rags and covered with chains; yet daring to raise his manacled hands to heaven, with a spirit soaring above the attributes of man; I looked on him and my blood curdled in my veins.

I will not shock the feelings of humanity, nor wound afresh the bosoms of the disconsolate sufferers in this unparalleled and inhuman massacre, by detailing the deeds of their fiend-like barbarity. There were two or three who were in the power of these wretches, had they known it, and who escaped in the most providential manner. There were two whom they thought they left dead on the field at Mr. Parker's, but who were only stunned by the blows of their guns, as they did not take time to re-load when they charged on them. The escape of a little girl who went to school at Mr. Waller's, and where the children were collecting for that purpose, excited general sympathy. As their teacher had not arrived, they were at play in the yard, and seeing the negroes approach, she ran up on a dirt chimney, (such as are common to log houses), and remained there unnoticed during the massacre of the eleven that were killed at this place. She remained on her hiding place till just before the arrival of a party, who were in pursuit of the murderers, when she came down and fled to a swamp, where, a mere child as she was, with the horrors of the late scene before her, she lay concealed until the next day, when seeing a party go up to the house, she came up, and on being asked how she escaped, replied with the utmost simplicity, "The Lord helped her." She was taken up behind a gentleman of the party, and returned to the arms of her weeping mother. Miss Whitehead concealed herself between the bed and the mast that supported it, while they murdered her sister in the same room, without discovering her. She was afterwards carried off, and concealed for protection by a slave of the family, who gave evidence against several of them on their trial. Mrs. Nathaniel Francis, while concealed in a closet heard their blows, and the shrieks of the victims of these ruthless savages; they then entered the closet where she was concealed, and went out without discovering her. While in this hiding place, she heard two of her women in a quarrel about the division of her clothes. Mr. John T. Barron, discovering them approaching his house, told his wife to make her escape, and scorning to fly, fell fighting on his own threshold. After firing his rifle, he discharged his gun at them, and then broke it over the villain who first approached him, but he was overpowered, and slain. His bravery, however, saved from the hands of these monsters, his lovely and amiable wife, who will long lament a husband so deserving of her love. As directed by him, she attempted to escape through the garden when she was caught and held by one of her servant girls, but another coming to her rescue, she fled to the woods, and concealed herself. Few indeed, were those who escaped their work of death. But fortunate for society, the hand of retributive justice has overtaken them; and not one that was known to be concerned has escaped.

After the "confession" is read to the court, Nat Turner is condemned to die:

The Commonwealth vs. Nat Turner.

Charged with making insurrection, and plotting to take away the lives of divers free white persons, &c. on the 22d of August, 1831. The court composed of _____ , having met for the trial of Nat Turner, the prisoner was brought in and arraigned, and upon his arraignment pleaded *Not guilty*; saying to his counsel, that he did not feel so.

On the part of the Commonwealth, Levi Waller was introduced, who being sworn, deposed as follows: (agreeably to Nat's own Confession.) Col. Trezvant[2] was then introduced, who being sworn, narrated Nat's Confession to him, as follows: (his Confession as given to Mr. Gray.) The prisoner introduced no evidence, and the case was submitted without argument to the court, who having found him guilty, Jeremiah Cobb, Esq. Chairman, pronounced the sentence of the court, in the following words: "Nat Turner! Stand up. Have you any thing to say why sentence of death should not be pronounced against you?"

Answer: I have not, I have made a full confession to Mr. Gray, and I have nothing more to say.

Attend then to the sentence of the Court. You have been arraigned and tried before this court, and convicted of one of the highest crimes in our criminal code. You have been convicted of plotting in cold blood, the indiscriminate destruction of men, of helpless women, and of infant children. The evidence before us leaves not a shadow of doubt, but that your hands were often imbrued in the blood of the innocent; and your own confession tells us that they were stained with the blood of a master; in your own language, "too indulgent." Could I stop here, your crime would be sufficiently aggravated. But the original contriver of a plan, deep and deadly, one that never can be effected, you managed so far to put it into execution, as to deprive us of many of our most valuable citizens; and this was done when they were asleep, and defenceless; under circumstances shocking to humanity. And while upon this part of the subject, I cannot but call your attention to the poor misguided wretches who have gone before you. They are not few in number—they were your bosom associates; and the blood of all cries aloud, and calls upon you,

---

[2] The committing magistrate.

as the author of their misfortune. Yes! You forced them unprepared, from Time to Eternity. Borne down by this load of guilt, your only justification is, that you were led away by fanaticism. If this be true, from my soul I pity you; and while you have my sympathies, I am, nevertheless called upon to pass the sentence of the court. The time between this and your execution, will necessarily be very short; and your only hope must be in another world. The judgment of the court is, that you be taken hence to the jail from whence you came, thence to the place of execution, and on Friday next, between the hours of 10 A.M. and 2 P.M. be hung by the neck until you are dead! dead! dead and may the Lord have mercy upon your soul.

QUESTIONS FOR RESPONSIVE ESSAYS

1. Paint as complete a portrait of Nat Turner as is possible from his own words and the established facts. What conditions do you feel motivated him to plan and lead his rebellion? What personal characteristics and life experiences made him the individual to lead such a rebellion? What strengths and weaknesses do you see in his character and reasoning that made him at first succeed but ultimately fail?

2. Describe Nat Turner's plan of action in the rebellion. In what ways did he make a realistic assessment of conditions, and in what ways was he unrealistic? How do you account for both? What mistakes led to the failure of his uprising?

3. Speculate on the trustworthiness of Gray's manuscript, which purports to be Nat's confession. Even if Nat dictated it and acknowledged its accuracy, how might the white secretary have guided the story and slanted its conclusions? To what extent is it a defendant's confession, and to what extent is it a prosecution document? Defend your opinion.

PART III

Immediate Reactions to the Turner Insurrection

Immediate reactions to Nat Turner's insurrection—from the southern press, from the slave population of Virginia, from northern abolitionists, and, finally, from politicians—were predictable and were as varied as the American populace. In Virginia and the rest of the South the insurrection produced shock and fear. Whites saw it as a mindless, undeserved attack upon innocent citizens by a crazed mob. Slaves were less surprised but braced themselves for reprisals against their black community. Northern abolitionists, led by the highly vocal editor William Lloyd Garrison, commented that a society such as that in the South, which tolerated the evil institution of slavery, should expect this kind of uprising. Politicians in Virginia and farther south began preparing what they considered to be appropriate public response. For all of them, however, Nat Turner was immediately established as a symbol: the slave who cried freedom. It is only in their evaluations of his bold act that they differed.

THE SOUTHERN PRESS

Although the editorial outlook of the southern press was not monolithic, the following report by the Richmond, Virginia, *Enquirer* on

August 30, 1831, reflects the general dismay, puzzlement, and fear that the Turner uprising provoked in the South:

THE BANDITTI

So much curiosity has been excited in the state, and so much exaggeration will go abroad, that we have determined to devote a great portion of this day's paper to the strange events in the county of Southampton. What strikes us as the most remarkable thing in this matter is the horrible ferocity of these monsters. They remind one of a parcel of blood-thirsty wolves rushing down from the Alps; or rather like a former incursion of the Indians upon the white settlements. Nothing is spared; neither age nor sex is respected—the helplessness of women and children pleads in vain for mercy. The danger is thought to be over—but prudence still demands precaution. The lower country should be on the alert.—The case of Nat Turner warns us. No black man ought to be permitted to turn a preacher through the country. The law must be enforced or the tragedy of Southampton appeals to us in vain.

* * *

Extract of a letter from Jerusalem, Va., 24th August, 3 o'clock.

The oldest inhabitants of our county have never experienced such a distressing time, as we have had since Sunday night last. The negroes, about fifteen miles from this place, have massacred from 50 to 75 women and children, and some 8 or 10 men. Every house, room and corner in this place is full of women and children, driven from home, who had to take the woods, until they could get to this place. We are worn out with fatigue.

* * *

A fanatic preacher by the name of Nat Turner (Gen. Nat Turner) who had been taught to read and write, and permitted to go about preaching in the country, was at the bottom of this infernal brigandage. He was artful, impudent and vindicative, without any cause or provocation, that could be assigned.—He was the slave of Mr. Travis. He and another slave of Mr. T. a young fellow, by the name of Moore, were two of the leaders. Three or four others were first concerned and most active.—They had 125 others to join them. And by importunity or threats they prevailed upon about 20 others to cooperate in the scheme of massacre. We cannot say how long they were organizing themselves—but they turned out on last Monday early (the 22d) upon their nefarious expedition. . . . They were mounted to the number of 40 or 50; and with knives and axes—knocking on the head, or cutting the throats of their victims. They had few firearms among them—and scarcely one, if one, was fit for use. . . . But as they went from house to house, they drank ardent spirits—and it is supposed, that in consequence of their being intoxicated, or from mere fatigue, they paused in their murderous career about 12 o'clock on Monday.

A fact or two, before we continue our narrative. These wretches are now estimated to have committed *sixty-one murders!* Not a white person escaped at all the houses they visited except *two.* One was a little child at Mrs. Waller's, about 7 or 8 years of age, who had sagacity enough to creep up a chimney; and the other was Mrs. Barrow, whose husband was murdered in his cotton patch, though he had received some notice in the course of the morning of the murderous deeds that were going on; but placed no confidence in the story and fell victim to his incredulity. His wife hid herself between weatherboarding, and the unplastered lathing, and escaped, the wretches not taking time to hunt her out. It was believed that one of the brigands had taken up a spit against Mr. Barrow, because he had refused him one of his female slaves for a wife.

Early on Tuesday morning, they attempted to renew their bloody work.—They made an attack upon Mr. Blunt, a gentleman who was very unwell with the gout, and who instead of flying determined to brave them out. He had several pieces of firearms, perhaps seven or eight, and had put them into the hands of his own slaves, who nobly and gallantly stood by him. They repelled the brigands—killed one, wounded and took prisoner (Gen. Moore), and we believe took a third who was not wounded at all. . . .

The militia of Southampton had been most active in ferreting out the fugitives from their hiding places. . . . But it deserves to be said to the credit of many of the slaves whom gratitude had bound to their masters, that they had manifested the greatest alacrity in detecting and apprehending many of the brigands. They had brought in several and a fine spirit had been shown in many of the plantations of confidence on the part of the masters, and gratitude on that of the slaves. It is said that from 40 to 50 blacks were in jail—some of whom were known to be concerned with the murders, and others suspected. The courts will discriminate the innocent from the guilty.

It is believed that all the brigands were slaves—and most, if not all these, the property of kind and indulgent masters. It is not known that any of them had been the runaways of the swamps and only one of them was a free man of color. He had afterwards returned to his own house, and a party sent there to apprehend him. He was accidently seen concealed in his yard and shot. . . .

Nat, the ringleader, who calls himself General, pretends to be a Baptist preacher—a great enthusiast—declares to his comrades that he is commissioned by Jesus Christ, and proceeds under his inspired directions—that the late singular appearance of the sun was the sign of him, etc., etc., is among the number not yet taken. The story of his having been killed at the bridge, and of two engagements there, is ungrounded. It is believed he cannot escape.

THE MEMORIES OF HARRIET JACOBS

It is difficult to assess how the slave population reacted to the Turner uprising. Only a few autobiographies by slaves then living have survived; most of them were written years after the uprising; and some slaves may have feared to comment on a violent event. Thus the memories of Harriet Jacobs are highly important. She was eighteen in 1831; and although her *Incidents in the Life of a Slave Girl* were not published until 1861, she provides us with one of the few frank accounts of slave reaction to Nat Turner's uprising.

Harriet Jacobs was born in Edenton, North Carolina, in 1813. Early in her life orphaned, she was sexually abused by both black and white men until in 1835 she ran way with her two children. For two years she hid in her grandmother's house, where to pass the time she sewed, read, and taught herself to write clear, precise prose. In 1842 she made her way to New York, then Boston, and even to England before settling in Rochester, New York, to work on Frederick Douglass' newspaper, the *North Star.* There she wrote the following account of the 1831 uprising:

Not far from home this time Nat Turner's insurrection broke out; and the news threw our town into great commotion. Strange that they should be alarmed, when their slaves were so "contented and happy"! But so it was.

It was always the custom to have a muster every year. On that occasion every white man shouldered his musket. The citizens and the so-called country gentlemen wore military uniforms. The poor whites took their places in the ranks in everyday dress, some without shoes, some without hats. This grand occasion had already passed; and when the slaves were told there was to be another muster, they were surprised and rejoiced. Poor creatures! They thought it was going to be a holiday. I was informed of the true state of the affairs, and imparted it to the few I could trust. Most gladly would I have proclaimed it to every slave; but I dared not. All could not be relied on. Mighty is the power of the torturing lash.

By sunrise, people were pouring in from every quarter within twenty miles of the town. I knew the houses were to be searched; and I expected it would be done by country bullies and the poor whites. I knew nothing annoyed them so much as to see colored people living in comfort and respectability; so I made arrangements for them with especial care. I arranged every thing in my grandmother's house as neatly as possible. I put white quilts on the beds, and decorated some of the rooms with flowers. When all was arranged I sat down at the window to watch. Far as my eye could reach, it rested on a motley crowd of soldiers. Drums and fifes were discoursing martial music. The men were divided into companies of sixteen, each headed by a captain. Orders were given, and the wild scouts rushed in every direction, wherever a colored face was to be found.

It was a grand opportunity for the low whites, who had no negroes of their own to scourge. They exulted in such a chance to exercise a little brief authority, and show their subserviency to the slaveholders; not reflecting that the power which trampled on the colored people also kept themselves in poverty, ignorance, and moral degradation. Those who never witnessed such scenes can hardly believe what I know was inflicted at this time on innocent men, women, and children, against whom there was not the slightest ground for suspicion. Colored people and slaves who lived in remote parts of the town suffered in an especial manner. In some cases the searchers scattered powder and shot among their clothes, and then sent other parties to find them, and bring them forward as proof that they were plotting insurrection. Everywhere men, women, and children were whipped till the blood stood in puddles at their feet. Some received five hundred lashes; others were tied hands and feet, and tortured with a bucking paddle, which blisters the skin terribly. The dwellings of the colored people, unless they happened to be protected by some influential white person, who was nigh at hand, were robbed of clothing and every thing else the marauders thought worth carrying away. All day long these unfeeling wretches went round, like a troop of demons, terrifying and tormenting the helpless. At night, they formed themselves into patrol bands, and went wherever they chose among the colored people, acting out their brutal will. Many women hid themselves in woods and swamps, to keep out of their way. If any of the husbands or fathers told of these outrages, they were tied up to the public whipping post, and cruelly scourged for telling lies about white men. The consternation was universal. No two people that had the slightest tinge of color in their faces dared to be seen talking together.

I entertained no positive fears about our household, because we were in the midst of white families who would protect us. We were ready to receive the soldiers whenever they came. It was not long before we heard the tramp of feet and the sound of voices. The door was rudely pushed open; and in they tumbled, like a pack of hungry wolves. They snatched at every thing within their reach. Every box, trunk, closet, and corner underwent a thorough examination. A box in one of the drawers containing some silver change was eagerly pounced upon. When I stepped forward to take it from them, one of the soldiers turned and said angrily, "What d'ye foller us fur? D'ye s'pose white folks is come to steal?"

I replied, "You have come to search; but you have searched that box, and I will take it, if you please."

At that moment I saw a white gentleman who was friendly to us; and I called to him, and asked him to have the goodness to come in and stay till the search was over. He readily complied. His entrance into the house brought in the captain of the company, whose business it was to guard the outside of the house, and see that none of the inmates left it. This officer was Mr. Litch, the wealthy slaveholder whom I mentioned, in the account of neighboring planters, as being notorious for his cruelty. He felt above soiling his hands with the search. He merely gave orders; and, if a bit of writing was discovered, it was carried to him by his ignorant followers, who were unable to read.

My grandmother had a large trunk of bedding and table cloths. When that was opened, there was a great shout of surprise; and one exclaimed, "Where'd the damned niggers git all dis sheet an' table clarf?"

My grandmother, emboldened by the presence of our white protector, said, "You may be sure we didn't pilfer 'em from *your* houses."

"Look here, mammy," said a grim-looking fellow without any coat, "you seem to feel mighty gran' 'cause you got all them 'ere fixens. White folks oughter have 'em all."

His remarks were interrupted by a chorus of voices shouting, "We's got 'em! We's got 'em! Dis 'ere yaller gal's got letters!"

There was a general rush for the supposed letter, which, upon examination, proved to be some verses written to me by a friend. In packing away my things, I had overlooked them. When their captain informed them of their contents, they seemed much disappointed.

He inquired of me who wrote them. I told him it was one of my friends. "Can you read them?" he asked. When I told him I could, he swore and raved, and tore the paper into bits. "Bring me all your letters!" said he, in a commanding tone. I told him I had none. "Don't be afraid," he continued, in an insinuating way. "Bring them all to me. Nobody shall do you any harm." Seeing I did not move to obey him his pleasant tone changed to oaths and threats. "Who writes to you? half free niggers?" inquired he. I replied, "O, no; most of my letters are from white people. Some request me to burn them after they are read, and some I destroy without reading."

An exclamation of surprise from some of the company put a stop to our conversation. Some silver spoons which ornamented an old-fashioned buffet had just been discovered. My grandmother was in the habit of preserving fruit for many ladies in town, and preparing suppers for parties; consequently she had many jars of preserves. The closet that contained these was next invaded, and the contents tasted. One of them, who was helping himself freely, tapped his neighbor on the shoulder, and said, "Wal done! Don't wonder de niggers want to kill all de white folks, when dey live on 'sarves." I stretched out my hand to take the jar, saying, "You were not here to search of sweetmeats."

"And what *were* we sent for?" said the captain, bristling up to me. I evaded the question.

The search of the house was completed, and nothing found to condemn us. They next proceeded to the garden, and knocked about every bush and vine, with no better success. The captain called his men together, and, after a short consultation, the order to march was given. As they passed out of the gate, the captain turned back, and pronounced a malediction on the house. He said it ought to be burned to the ground, and each of its inmates receive thirty-nine lashes. We came out of this affair very fortunately; not losing any thing except some wearing apparel.

Towards evening the turbulence increased. The soldiers, stimulated by drink, committed still greater cruelties. Shrieks and shouts continually rent the air. Not daring to go to the door, I peeped under the window curtain. I saw a mob dragging along a number of colored people, each white man, with his musket upraised, threatening instant death if they did not stop their shrieks. Among the prisoners was a respectable old colored minister. They had found a few parcels of shot in his house, which his wife had for years used to balance her scales. For this they were going to shoot him on Court House Green.

What a spectacle was that for a civilized country! A rabble, staggering under intoxication, assuming to be the administrators of justice!

The better class of the community exerted their influence to save the innocent, persecuted people; and in several instances they succeeded, by keeping them shut up in jail till the excitement abated. At last the white citizens found that their own property was not safe from the lawless rabble they had summoned to protect them. They rallied the drunken swarm, drove them back into the country, and set a guard over the town.

The next day, the town patrols were commissioned to search colored people that lived out of the city; and the most shocking outrages were committed with perfect impunity. Every day for a fortnight, if I looked out, I saw horsemen with some poor panting negro tied to their saddles, and compelled by the lash to keep up with their speed, till they arrived at the jail yard. Those who had been whipped too unmercifully to walk were washed with brine, tossed into a cart, and carried to jail. One black man, who had not fortitude to endure scourging, promised to give information about the conspiracy. But it turned out that he knew nothing at all. He has not even heard the name of Nat Turner. The poor fellow had, however, made up a story, which augmented his own sufferings and those of the colored people.

The day patrol continued for some weeks, and at sundown a night guard was substituted. Nothing at all was proved against the colored people, bond or free. The wrath of the slaveholders was somewhat appeased by the capture of Nat Turner. The imprisoned were released. The slaves were sent to their masters, and the free were permitted to return to their ravaged homes. Visiting was strictly forbidden on the plantations. The slaves begged the privilege of again meeting at their little church in the woods, with their burying ground around it. It was built by the colored people, and they had no higher happiness than to meet there and sing hymns together, and pour out their hearts in spontaneous prayer. Their request was denied, and the church was demolished. They were permitted to attend the white churches, a certain portion of the galleries being appropriated to their use. There, when every body else had partaken of the communion, and the benediction had been pronounced, the minister said, "Come down, now, my colored friends." They obeyed the summons, and partook of the bread and wine, in commemoration of the meek and lowly Jesus, who said, "God is your Father, and all ye are brethren."

WILLIAM LLOYD GARRISON'S INDICTMENT

The most prominent northern abolitionist, William Lloyd Garrison, was just beginning his crusade to free American slaves when Nat Turner led his insurrection. Garrison's controversial newspaper, the *Liberator,* had first appeared in January 1831, just eight months before the insurrection in Virginia. Garrison would go on for many years to be one of the leading white opponents of what he considered the South's evil practice of slavery. Whereas many white leaders, especially politicians such as Henry Clay, suggested that slavery be slowly and supposedly less painfully eliminated, Garrison and other abolitionists argued that it must end immediately and that each day it continued soiled the nation more deeply.

To Garrison and the readers of his paper the Nat Turner uprising was the natural result of slavery's oppression, and Nat was both a man and a symbol of resistance to its injustice. The following editorial appeared in the *Liberator*'s September 3, 1831, edition:

What we have long predicted,—at the peril of being stigmatized as an alarmist and declaimer,—has commenced its fulfillment. The first step of the earthquake, which is ultimately to shake down the fabric of oppression, leaving not one stone upon the other, has been made. The first drops of blood, which are but the prelude to a deluge from the gathering clouds, have fallen. The first flash of lightning, which is to ignite and consume, has been felt. The first wailings of a bereavement, which is to clothe the earth in sackcloth, have broken upon our ears.

In the first number of the *Liberator,* we alluded to the hour of vengence in the following lines:

> Wo if it comes with storm, and blood, and fire,
> When midnight darkness veils the earth and sky!
> *Wo to the innocent babe*—the guilty sire—
> *Mother and daughter*—friends of kindred tie
> *Stranger and citizen alike shall die!*
> Red-handed Slaughter his revenge shall feed,
> And Havoc yell his ominous death-cry,
> And wild Despair in vain for Mercy plead,—
> While hell itself shall shrink and sicken at the deed!

Read the account of the insurrection in Virginia, and say whether our prophecy be not fulfilled. What was poetry—imagination—in January, is now a bloody reality. . . . Turn again to the record of slaughter! Whole families have been cut off—not a mother, not a daughter, not a babe left. Dreadful retaliation! "The dead bodies of white and black lying just as they were slain, unburied"—the oppressor and the oppressed equal at last in death—what a spectacle!

True, the rebellion is quelled. Those of the slaves who were not killed in combat, have been secured, and the prison is crowded with victims destined for the gallows! Yet laugh not in your carnival of crime too proudly, ye oppressors!

You have seen, it is to be feared, but the beginning of sorrows. All the blood which has been shed will be required at your hands. At your hands alone? No—but at the hands of the people of New-England and of all the free states. The crime of oppression is national. The South is only the agent in this guilty traffic. But, remember! The same causes are at work which must inevitably produce the same effects; and when the contest shall have again begun, it must be a war of extermination. In the present instance, no quarters have been asked or given.

But we have killed and routed them now—we can do it again—we are invincible! A dastardly triumph, well becoming a nation of oppressors. Detestable complacency, that can think, without emotion, of the extermination of the blacks! We have the power to kill all—let us, therefore, continue to apply the whip and forge new fetters!

In his fury against the revolters, who will remember their wrongs? What will it avail them, though the catalogue of their sufferings, dripping with warm blood fresh from their lacerated bodies, be held up to extenuate their conduct? It is enough that the victims were black—that circumstances made them less precious than the dogs which have been slain in our streets! They were black-brutes, pretending to be men—legions of curses on their memories! They were black—God made them to serve us!

Ye patriotic hypocrites! ye panegyrists of Frenchmen, Greeks and Poles! ye fustian declaimers for liberty! ye valient sticklers for equal rights among yourselves! ye haters of aristocracy! ye assailants of monarchies! ye republican nullifiers! ye treasonable disunionists! ye dumb! Cast no reproach upon the conduct of the slaves, but let your lips and cheeks wear the blisters of condemnation!

Ye accuse the pacific friends of emancipation of instigating the slaves to revolt. Take back the charge as foul slander. The slaves need no incentive at our hands. They will find in their stripes—in their emaciated bodies—in their ceaseless toil—in their ignorant minds—in every field, in every valley, on every hill top and mountain, wherever you and your fathers have fought for liberty—in your speeches and conversations, your celebrations, your pamphlets, your newspapers— voices in the air, sounds from across the ocean, invitations to resistance above, below, around them! What more do they need! Surrounded by such influences, and smarting under the newly made wounds, is it wonderful that they should rise to contend—as other "heroes" have contended—for their lost rights? It is *not* wonderful.

In all that we have written, is there aught to justify the excesses of the slaves? No. Nevertheless, they deserve no more censure than the Greeks in destroying the Turks, or the Poles in exterminating the Russians, or our fathers in slaughtering the British. Dreadful, indeed, is the standard erected by worldly patriotism!

For ourselves, we are horror-struck at the late tidings. We have exerted our utmost efforts to avert the calamity. We have warned our countrymen of the danger of persisting in their unrighteous conduct. We have preached to the slaves the pacific precepts of Jesus Christ. We have appealed to christians, philanthropists and patriots, for their assistance to accomplish the great work of national redemption through the agency of moral power—of public opinion—of individual duty. How have we been received? We have been threatened, proscribed, vilified and imprisoned—a laughing stock and a reproach. . . . If we have been hitherto urgent, and bold, and denunciatory in our efforts—hereafter we shall grow vehement and active with the increase of danger. We shall cry, in trumpet tones, night and day,— Wo to this guilty land, unless she speedily repents of her evil doings! The blood of millions of her sons cries aloud for redress! IMMEDIATE EMANCIPATION can alone save her from the vengence of Heaven, and cancel the debt of ages!

Two weeks later, on September 17, Garrison printed in the *Liberator* the following letter, which also reflected his own views:

Sir—I have sometimes heard people say that if it had not been for the *Liberator,* the slaves in Virginia would have been quiet. Opinions of this kind are uttered with the greatest gravity and confidence by persons who have never seen the *Liberator,* and in the absence of all evidence that any of the persons concerned in the late sanguinary proceedings in Virginia had ever read the paper.

The truth is that men are too ready to ascribe sudden and violent eruptions of evil to the operation of temporary causes. Everyone is more ready to charge any sickness under which he may be suffering to some accident, rather than to a decaying constitution; he is willing to flatter himself that his malady is not deeply rooted in his frame.

There would, perhaps, be some show of justice in charging the recent insurrection to the *Liberator,* if no other obvious and sufficient causes of such risings could be pointed out, or if this were the first occasion on which slaves had risen against their masters. But, sir, the causes of negro insurrections may be discovered without any deep research, they obtrude themselves upon our observation.

Negroes, like other men, have a spirit which rebels against tyranny and oppression. It is their wrongs and sufferings which have driven them to the unjustifiable measures which we now observe. Let any unprejudiced person read the law, which serve the practice of slavery in the Southern States, and he will only wonder that they are not more frequent. . . . Let the stranger then heed to the military music of the armed watch which is kept all night in the city; and in case of an alarm of fire by day or night, let him watch the citizens rushing from their houses armed with muskets and cartridge boxes, and then let him ask himself whether slaveholders do not anticipate insurrections among their slaves? And as these precautions were taken long before the *Liberator* was established, may he not conclude that symptoms of disaffection also existed among the slaves before that time?

Other obvious causes of insurrection might easily be pointed out; but I shall only advert to one. This is a land of freedom. Nothing can prevent the slaves from hearing conversation and declamations of liberty and the rights of man. They perceive our annual celebration on the fourth of July. Can they fail to learn something of its causes? Do not our boastings of our resistance to British oppression sometimes reach their ears? Are they deaf to the sympathizing applause which the accounts of the noble resistance of Poland to Russian despotism, have been received in America? It cannot be. Even if they had less of a human nature than the whites, even if they were not keenly sensible of their wrongs, they would soon learn from their masters how to prize freedom.

But sir, everyone who is at all familiar with history, ancient or modern, must be aware that conspiracies and insurrections have always been frequent among slaves. They are the natural fruit of oppression. . . . Hundreds of such . . . have probably occurred long before the invention of printing, and in places where newspapers never circulated. For slaveholders then to ascribe the recent disturbance in Virginia to the *Liberator,* seems very much like the charge of the wolf against the lamb of muddying the stream from which he was drinking, when she was standing at a point below him. It is as unreasonable to call the *Liberator* the author of the outrages of the blacks, because it has endeavored to warn the southern people of their danger, as it would be to charge a man with having set fire to your house, because he woke you and told you that it was in flames.

GOVERNOR JOHN FLOYD BEFORE THE VIRGINIA LEGISLATURE

Southern politicians—as well as politicians in other parts of the nation who might in the future need southern support—carefully weighed their responses to the Turner uprising. And nowhere was the response more carefully weighed than in Virginia, where the proper response to white fears and desire for revenge was of the highest political importance. On December 6, 1831, Virginia's Governor John Floyd addressed a joint session of the Virginia Legislature to give his assessment of the uprising and to recommend measures to assure that it not be repeated. There had been in recent years a small but articulate movement among some Virginians to phase out slavery in the state; but the Turner uprising changed the political atmosphere both in Virginia and throughout the South. The following is in part what Governor Floyd said to his "Fellow-Citizens of the Senate and of the House of Delegates":

Whilst we were enjoying the abundance of the last season, reposing in the peace and quiet of domestic comfort and safety—we were suddenly aroused from that security by receiving information, that a portion of our fellow-citizens had fallen victims to the relentless fury of assassins and murderers, even whilst wrapped in profound sleep and that, those bloody deeds had been perpetrated in a spirit of wantonness and cruelty, unknown to savage warfare even in their most revolting form.

In August last, a banditti of slaves, consisting of but few at first, and not at any time exceeding a greater number than seventy, rose upon some of the unsuspecting and defenceless inhabitants of Southampton, and under circumstances of the most shocking and horrid barbarity, put to death sixty-one persons, of whom, the greater number were women and helpless children.—Much of this bloody work was done on Monday morning, and on the day following, about ten o'clock, the last murder was committed.—The citizens of that and the adjacent counties, promptly assembled, and all real danger was speedily terminated.

* * *

All of those who participated in the bloody tragedy, have expiated their crimes by undergoing public execution, whilst some who had been condemned have been reprieved for reasons which were deemed satisfactory.—There is much reason to believe the spirit of insurrection was not confined to Southampton; many convictions have taken place elsewhere, and some few in distant counties. From the documents which I herewith lay before you, there is too much reason to believe those plans of treason, insurrection and murder, have been designed, planned and matured by unrestrained fanatics in some of the neighbouring States, who find facilities in distributing their views and plans amongst our population, either through the Post Office, or by Agents sent for that purpose throughout our territory.

Upon inspecting these documents, and contemplating that state of things which they are intended to produce, I felt it my duty to open a correspondence with the Governors of some of the neighbouring powers of this confederacy, to preserve as far as possible the good understanding which exists, and which ought to be cherished between the different members of this Union. The result of this correspondence will be made known to you, so soon as it is ascertained.

The most active among ourselves, in stirring up the spirit of revolt, have been the negro preachers. They had acquired great ascendancy over the minds of their fellows, and infused all their opinions, which had prepared them for the development of the final design. There is also some reason to believe, those preachers have a perfect understanding in relation to these plans throughout the Eastern counties— and have been the channels through which the inflammatory papers and pamphlets, brought here by the agents and emissaries from other States, have been circulated amongst our slaves. The facilities thus afforded for plotting treason and conspiracy to rebel and make insurrection, have been great: Through the indulgence of the magistracy and the laws, large collections of slaves have been permitted to take place, at any time through the week, for the ostensible purpose of indulging in religious worship, but in many instances, the real purpose, with the preacher, was of a different character; the sentiments, and sometimes the words of these inflammatory pamphlets, which the meek and charitable of other States have seen cause to distribute as fire-brands in the bosom of our society, have been read. What shall be thought of those fiends, who, having no interest in our community, nevertheless seek to excite a servile war—a war which exhausts itself in the massacre of unoffending women and children on the one side, and on the other, in the sacrifice of all who have borne part in the savage undertaking? Not only should the severest punishment be inflicted upon those disturbers of our peace whenever they or their emissaries are found within our reach, but decisive measures should be adopted to make all their measures abortive. The public good requires the negro preachers to be silenced, who, full of ignorance, are incapable of inculcating any thing but notions of the wildest superstition, thus preparing fit instruments in the hands of the crafty agitators, to destroy the public tranquility.

As the means of guarding against the possible repetition of these sanguinary scenes, I cannot fail to recommend to your early attention, the revision of all the laws intended to preserve in due subordination the slave population of our State. In urging these considerations upon you, let me not be understood as expressing the slightest doubt or apprehension of general results; all communities are liable to suffer from the dagger of the murderer and midnight assassin; and it behooves them to guard against them.

With us the first returning light dispels the danger, and soon witnesses the murderer in chains.

Though means have been taken by those of other States to agitate our community and discontent our slaves and incite them to attempt an unattainable object, some proof is also furnished, that for the class of free people of colour, they have opened more enlarged views, and urge the achievement of a higher destiny, by means, for the present less violent, but not differing in the end from those presented to the slaves. That class of the community, our laws have heretofore treated with indulgent kindness, and many instances of solicitude for their welfare have marked the progress of legislation.—If the slave is confined by law to the estate of his master, as it is advisable he should be, the free people of colour may nevertheless convey all the incendiary pamphlets and papers, with which we are sought to be inundated. This class too, has been the first to place itself in hostile array against any and every measure designed to remove them from amongst us. Though it will be indispensably necessary for them to withdraw from this community, yet in the spirit of kindness, which has ever characterized the legislature of Virginia, it is submitted, whether as the last benefit which we can confer upon them, it may not be wise to appropriate annually a sum of money to aid in their removal from this Commonwealth.

Whilst recent events had created apprehensions in the minds of a few, some agitation was also more extensively felt; wherefore, it was deemed prudent to arm the militia in a manner calculated to quiet all apprehensions, and arms were accordingly furnished to nearly all the regiments on the Eastern frontier. The want of them, upon this sudden emergency, was so sensibly felt by those in the vicinity of Norfolk, as to induce Commodore Warrington, in command of the Navy Yard in Gosport, to distribute a portion of the public arms under his care. That gallant and patriotic officer, did not hesitate to assume the responsibility of this step, and it is gratifying to perceive that his conduct has met the approbation of the public functionaries.—The policy of disarming the militia, it is believed, was pursued as a measure of economy, as the men and officers had been culpably negligent in their attention to their preservation, so that many were lost, or by neglect become unfit for service. Now, however, the necessity for preserving them is distinctly felt, and a doubt cannot be entertained, that more care will be taken of them in future. I could not weigh the expense incurred by this measure, against the possible sacrifice of life, much less the possible repetition of the scenes of Southampton. . . .

It will be necessary to call your attention to the present condition of our militia, and to recommend a thorough revision of the law on that subject. Much of the strength and efficiency of that kind of force depends upon the promptness with which they can be ready for action, and some knowledge of the first duties of a soldier.

Our light troops might be increased in every battalion and regiment with great advantage to the service, and ought to be encouraged by privileges and exemptions, as they will always be the first called into service, and unlike the infantry of the line, they will be called out by whole companies instead of being detailed for duty as is now the case with the body of the militia. From the dexterity and skill of our citizens in the use of the rifle, and a fondness for that kind of arms, as well as the great care and time it requires to drill a regiment in the rifle exercise, the property of organizing them into regiments is suggested.

From the position in which this State is placed, and the attitude occupied by her, it becomes a matter of very serious reflection, whether a force more available than the militia may not be advisable and attainable at a small expense. By a well organized intermediate force, even a foreign war might be sustained without disturbing the quiet operations of the Government, or of the farmer. We have at this time an hundred and thirty-nine regiments full and strong—Were one company to be authorized by law to be raised by voluntary enlistment from each regiment, or such number of regiments as would give the number of men required, and put upon the footing of the Public Guard, you would have a cheap and efficient army ready to perform any and every duty. These soldiers might be permitted to live at home and work their crops as heretofore, but at all times subject to the call of their officers. Some allowances should be made them, and the equipments of a soldier furnished as an inducement to enlist; to be drilled once a month for as many days as the General Assembly should think proper, and whilst on drill, to receive ample pay for their time, but no other pay allowed unless embodied for service, when their pay and allowances should be the same as that received by the Public Guard now in service.

It will be found, on inspection, that many of the public arms now in the Arsenal, need repair, particularly those of the smaller calibre, a part of which, by law, were intended to arm the twenty-first brigade— application has been made for the residue required for that purpose, but has been delayed, until this representation could be made to you: Nor can I refrain from calling your attention to the necessity of providing sword slings, cartouch boxes and holsters, of which at this time the militia are much in want, besides some equipments for the artillery. . . .

A NEW LAW CONCERNING SLAVERY IN VIRGINIA

On March 15, 1832, four months after the governor's address and more than half a year after Nat Turner's revolt, the legislature of Virginia passed a new law. It is clear that the revolt had changed the political climate in that state and that the new law sought to end the threat of further revolts. Other southern states would soon follow Virginia's lead, in some cases passing even more stringent measures than these to cope with the large slave populations among them:

1. *Be it enacted by the general assembly,* That no slave, free negro or mulatto, whether he shall have been ordained or licensed, or otherwise, shall hereafter undertake to preach, exhort or conduct, or hold any assembly or meeting, for religious or other purposes, either in the day time, or at night; and any slave, free negro or mulatto, so offending, shall for every such offence, be punished with stripes, at the discretion of any justice of the

peace, not exceeding thirty-nine lashes; and any person desiring so to do, shall have authority, without any previous written precept or otherwise, to apprehend any such offender and carry him before such justice.

2. Any slave, free negro or mulatto, who shall hereafter attend any preaching, meeting or other assembly, held or pretended to be held for religious purposes, or other instruction, conducted by any slave, free negro or mulatto preacher, ordained or otherwise; and any slave who shall hereafter attend any preaching in the night time, although conducted by a white minister, without a written permission from his or her owner, overseer or master or agent of either of them, shall be punished by stripes at the discretion of any justice of the peace, not exceeding thirty-nine lashes; and may for that purpose be apprehended by any person, without any written or other precept: *Provided,* That nothing herein contained shall be so construed, as to prevent the masters or owners of slaves, or any white person to whom any free negro or mulatto is bound, or in whose employment, or on whose plantation or lot such a free negro or mulatto lives, from carrying or permitting any such slave, free negro or mulatto, to go with him, her or them, or with any part of his, her, or their white family to any place of religious worship, conducted by a white minister, in the night time: *And provided also,* That nothing in this, or any former law, shall be so construed, as to prevent any ordained or licensed white minister of the gospel, or any layman licensed for that purpose by the denomination to which he may belong, from preaching, or giving religious instruction to slaves, free negroes and mulattoes, in the day time; nor to deprive any masters or owners of slaves of the right to engage, or employ any free white person whom they may think proper, to give religious instruction to their slaves; nor to prevent the assembling of the slaves of any one master together, at any time for religious devotion.

3. No free negro or mulatto shall hereafter be capable of purchasing or otherwise acquiring permanent ownership, except by descent, to any slave, other than his or her husband, wife or children; and all contracts for any such purchase are hereby declared to be null and void.

4. No free negro or mulatto shall be suffered to keep or carry any firelock of any kind, any military weapon, or any powder or lead; and any free negro or mulatto who shall so offend, shall, on conviction

before a justice of the peace, forfeit all such arms and ammunition to the use of the informer; and shall moreover be punished with stripes, at the discretion of the justice, not exceeding thirty-nine lashes. And the proviso to the seventh section of the act, entitled, "an act reducing into one of the several acts concerning slaves, free negroes and mulattoes," passed the second day of March, one thousand eight hundred and nineteenth, authorizing justices of the peace, in certain cases, to permit slaves to keep and use guns or other weapons, powder and shot; and so much of the eighth section of the said recited act as authorizes the county and corporation courts to grant licenses to free negroes and mulattoes to keep or carry any firelock of any kind, any military weapon, or any powder or lead, shall be, and the same are hereby repealed.

5. No slave, free negro or mulatto, shall hereafter be permitted to sell, give, or otherwise dispose of any ardent or spirituous liquor at or within one mile of any muster, preaching, or other public assembly of black or white persons; and any slave, free negro or mulatto, so offending, shall be punished by stripes, at the discretion of a justice of the peace, not exceeding thirty-nine.

6. If any slave, free negro or mulatto, shall hereafter wilfully and maliciously assault and beat any white person, with intention in so doing to kill such white person; every such slave, free negro or mulatto, so offending, and being thereof lawfully convicted, shall be adjudged and deemed guilty of felony, and shall suffer death without benefit of clergy.

7. If any person shall hereafter write, print, or cause to be written or printed, any book, pamphlet or other writing, advising persons of colour within this state to make insurrection, or to rebel, or shall knowingly circulate, or cause to be circulated, any book, pamphlet or other writing, written or printed, advising persons of colour in this commonwealth to commit insurrection or rebellion; such person if a slave, free negro or mulatto, shall, on conviction before any justice of the peace, be punished for the first offence with stripes, at the discretion of the said justice, not exceeding thirty-nine lashes; and for the second offence, shall be deemed guilty of felony, and on due conviction, shall be punished with death without benefit of clergy; and if the person so offending be a white person, he or she shall be punished on conviction, in a sum not less than one hundred nor more than one thousand dollars.

8. Riots, routs, unlawful assemblies, trespasses and seditious speeches, by free negroes or mulattoes, shall hereafter be punished with stripes, in the same mode, and to the same extent, as slaves are directed to be punished by the twelfth section of the before recited act. . . .

QUESTIONS FOR RESPONSIVE ESSAYS

1. What does Harriet Jacobs' reaction to the news that Nat Turner had led an insurrection in the neighboring state of Virginia tell you about the reaction of slaves in general to the news? How might her memory and interpretation of the event have been changed by the thirty years that passed between the event and her writing? How does her interpretation of the event differ from those of both southern and northern white journalists?

2. Compare how the Richmond *Enquirer* and Garrison's Boston *Liberator* reacted to the Turner insurrection. How do they differ in their assumptions about slavery and the causes of the insurrection? In what forms are the strains in North-South opinion and relations that will lead to the Civil War already evident in these commentaries?

3. Examine Governor Floyd's speech to the Virginia Legislature and the law that the legislature enacted for clues as to how southern officials read the public mood and decided how they must react to the Turner uprising. To what extent did their reactions succeed in suppressing slave restlessness, and to what extent did their reactions probably increase both slave resentment and determination to escape slavery? Suggest other reactions that might have been more and less effective than these by Virginia's officials.

PART IV

Further Reactions: Escape and Abolitionism

Nat Turner's uprising made him a symbolic figure for the American nation after 1831. The next attempted uprising came twenty-eight years later, when a white abolitionist named John Brown tried to take over a federal army arsenal at Harpers Ferry, Virginia, in 1859, contributing to the outbreak of the Civil War two years later. The brutal suppression of Nat Turner's uprising taught slaves that such actions were, without governmental support, as futile as they were heroic. But Nat's action also inspired more resistance to slavery than had been seen before. The resistance simply took other forms.

There had always been runaway slaves, but their numbers increased after the Turner uprising. Runaways who made it into the North, some going on to Canada and some to Britain, often told their stories to sympathetic audiences and committed their stories to writing. Most runaways happily joined the growing movement to abolish slavery in the United States. Nat Turner's spirit, his cry of freedom in America, lived on.

THE FLIGHT OF THE CRAFTS

Of all the stories reported by escaped slaves, none is more intriguing than that of a husband and wife, William and Ellen Craft, who ran away from bondage in Macon, Georgia, at Christmas, 1848. Their narrative is still thrilling today, a century and a half later. In the following passage from their life story, told in their own words, we learn the perils of escape, the courage it took, and the feeling of freedom it brought, when successful. Ellen Craft was of a light complexion, and so she dressed as a white man, a supposed slave owner, traveling north accompanied by her black slave, who was, in fact, her husband. After safely arriving in free territory, they eventually made their way to England because the Fugitive Slave Act of 1850 made life risky even in the North. In England they studied at a school founded by Lady Byron for the rural poor, and once literate they began writing their memoirs, which were published in London in the 1850s. Here is their story:

It is a fact worthy of remark, that nothing seems to give the slaveholders so much pleasure as the catching and torturing of fugitives. They had much rather take the keen and poisonous lash, and with it cut their poor trembling victims to atoms, than allow one of them to escape to a free country, and expose the infamous system from which he fled.

The greatest excitement prevails at a slavehunt. The slaveholders and their hired ruffians appear to take more pleasure in this inhuman pursuit than English sportsmen do in chasing a fox or a stag. Therefore, knowing what we should have been compelled to suffer, if caught and taken back, we were more than anxious to hit upon a plan that would lead us safely to a land of liberty.

But, after puzzling our brains for years, we were reluctantly driven to the sad conclusion, that it was almost impossible to escape from slavery in Georgia, and travel 1,000 miles across the slave States. We therefore resolved to get the consent of our owners, be married, settle down in slavery, and endeavor to make ourselves as comfortable as possible under that system; but at the same time ever to keep our dim eyes steadily fixed upon the glimmering hope of liberty, and earnestly pray God mercifully to assist us to escape from our unjust thraldom.

We were married, and prayed and toiled on till December 1848, at which time (as I have stated) a plan suggested itself that proved quite successful, and in eight days after it was first thought of we were free from the horrible trammels of slavery, and glorifying God who had brought us safely out of a land of bondage.

Knowing that slaveholders have the privilege of taking their slaves to any part of the country they think proper, it occurred to me that, as my wife was nearly white, I might get her to disguise herself as an invalid gentleman, and assume to be my master, while I could attend as his slave, and that in this manner we might effect our escape. After I thought of the plan, I suggested it to my wife, but at first she shrank from the idea. She thought it was almost impossible for her to assume that disguise, and travel a distance of 1,000 miles across the slave States. However, on the other hand, she also thought of her condition. She saw that the laws under which we lived did not recognize her to be a woman, but a mere chattel, to be bought and sold, or otherwise dealt with as her owner might see fit. Therefore the more she contemplated her helpless condition, the more anxious she was to escape from it. So she said, "I think it is almost too much for us to undertake; however, I feel that God is on our side, and with his assistance, notwithstanding all the difficulties, we shall be able to succeed. Therefore, if you will purchase the disguise, I will try to carry out the plan."

But after I concluded to purchase the disguise, I was afraid to go to anyone to ask him to sell me the articles. It is unlawful in Georgia for a white man to trade with slaves without the master's consent. But, notwithstanding this, many persons will sell a slave any article that he can get the money to buy. Not that they sympathize with the slave, but merely because his testimony is not admitted in court against a free white person.

Therefore, with little difficulty I went to different parts of the town, at odd times, and purchased things piece by piece (except the trousers which she found necessary to make) and took them home to the house where my wife resided. She being a ladies' maid, and a favorite slave in the family, was allowed a little room to herself; and amongst other pieces of furniture which I had made in my overtime, was a chest of drawers; so when I took the articles home, she locked them up carefully in these drawers. No one about the premises knew that she had anything of the kind. So when we fancied we had everything ready the time was fixed for the flight. But we knew it would not do to start off without first getting our masters' consent to be away for a few days. Had we left without this, they would soon have had us back into slavery, and probably we should never have got another fair opportunity of even attempting to escape.

* * *

When the time had arrived for us to start, we blew out the lights, knelt down, and prayed to our Heavenly Father mercifully to assist us, as he did his people of old, to escape from cruel bondage; and we shall ever feel that God heard and answered our prayer. Had we not been sustained by a kind, and I sometimes think special, providence, we could never have overcome the mountainous difficulties which I am now about to describe.

After this we rose and stood for a few moments in breathless silence—we were afraid that someone might have been about the cottage listening and watching our movements. So I took my wife by the hand, stepped softly to the door, raised the latch, drew it open, and peeped out. Though there were trees all around the house, yet the foliage scarcely moved; in fact, everything appeared to be as still as death. I then whispered to my wife, "Come my dear, let us make a desperate leap for liberty!" But poor thing, she shrank back, in a state of trepidation. I turned and asked what was the matter; she made no reply, but burst into violent sobs, and threw her head upon my breast. This appeared to touch my very heart, it caused me to enter into her feelings more fully than ever. We both saw the many mountainous difficulties that rose one after the other before our view, and knew far too well what our sad fate would have been, were we caught and forced back into our slavish den. Therefore on my wife's fully realizing the solemn fact that we had to take our lives, as it were, in our hands, and contest every inch of the thousand miles of slave territory over which we had to pass, it made her heart almost sink within her, and, had I known them at that time, I would have repeated the following encouraging lines, which may not be out of place here—

> The hill, though high, I covet to ascend,
> The difficulty will not offend;
> For I perceive the way to life lies here:
> Come, pluck up heart, let's neither faint nor fear;
> Better, though difficult, the right way to go,—
> Than wrong, though easy, where the end is woe.

However, the sobbing was soon over, and after a few moments of silent prayer she recovered her self-possession, and said, "Come, William, it is getting late, so now let us venture upon our perilous journey."

We then opened the door, and stepped as softly out as "moonlight upon the water." I locked the door with my own key, which I now have before me, and tiptoed across the yard into the street. I say tiptoed, because we were like persons near a tottering avalanche, afraid to move, or even breathe freely, for fear the sleeping tyrants should be aroused, and come down upon us with double vengeance, for daring to attempt to escape in the manner which we contemplated.

We shook hands, said farewell, and started in different directions for the railway station. I took the nearest possible way to the train, for fear I should be recognized by someone, and got into the Negro car in which I knew I should have to ride; but my *master* (as I will now call my wife) took a longer way round, and only arrived there with the bulk of the passengers. He obtained a ticket for himself and one for his slave to Savannah, the first port, which was about two hundred miles off. My master then had the baggage stowed away, and stepped into one of the best carriages.

But just before the train moved off I peeped through the window, and, to my great astonishment, I saw the cabinetmaker with whom I had worked so long, on the platform. He stepped up to the ticket-seller, and asked some question, and then commenced looking rapidly through the passengers, and into the carriages. Fully believing that we were caught, I shrank into a corner, turned my face from the door, and expected in a moment to be dragged out. The cabinetmaker looked into my master's carriage, but did not know him in his new attire, and, as God would have it, before he reached mine the bell rang, and the train moved off.

I have heard since that the cabinetmaker had a presentiment that we were about to "make tracks for parts unknown"; but, not seeing me, his suspicions vanished, until he received the startling intelligence that we had arrived safely in a free State.

As soon as the train had left the platform, my master looked round in the carriage, and was terror-stricken to find a Mr. Cray—an old friend of my wife's master, who dined with the family the day before, and knew my wife from childhood—sitting on the same seat.

The doors of the American railway carriages are at the ends. The passengers walk up the aisle, and take seats on either side; and as my master was engaged in looking out of the window, he did not see who came in.

My master's first impression, after seeing Mr. Cray, was, that he was there for the purpose of securing him. However, my master thought it was not wise to give any information respecting himself, and for fear that Mr. Cray might draw him into conversation and recognize his voice, my master resolved to feign deafness as the only means of self-defense.

After a little while, Mr. Cray said to my master, "It is a very fine morning, sir." The latter took no notice, but kept looking out of the window. Mr. Cray soon repeated this remark, in a little louder tone, but my master remained as before. This indifference attracted the attention of the passengers near, one of whom laughed out. This, I suppose, annoyed the old gentleman; so he said, "I will make him hear"; and in a loud tone of voice repeated, "It is a very fine morning, sir."

My master turned his head, and with a polite bow said, "Yes," and commenced looking out of the window again.

One of the gentlemen remarked that it was a very great deprivation to be deaf. "Yes," replied Mr. Cray, "and I shall not trouble that fellow any more." This enabled my master to breathe a little easier, and to feel that Mr. Cray was not his pursuer after all.

The gentlemen then turned the conversation upon the three great topics of discussion in first-class circles in Georgia, namely, Niggers, Cotton, and the Abolitionists.

* * *

On arriving [in Baltimore] we felt more anxious than ever, because we knew not what that last dark night would bring forth. It is true we were near the goal, but our poor hearts were still as if tossed at sea; and, as there was another great and dangerous bar to pass, we were afraid our liberties would be wrecked, and, like the ill-fated *Royal Charter,* [a recent shipwreck] go down forever just off the place we longed to reach.

They are particularly watchful at Baltimore to prevent slaves from escaping into Pennsylvania, which is a free State. After I had seen my master into one of the best carriages, and was just about to step into mine, an officer, a full-blooded Yankee of the lower order, saw me. He came quickly up, and, tapping me on the shoulder, said in his unmistakable native twang, together with no little display of his authority, "Where are you going, boy?" "To Philadelphia, sir," I humbly replied. "Well, what are you going there for?" "I am travelling with my master, who is in the next carriage, sir." "Well, I calculate you had better get him out; and be mighty quick about it, because the train will soon be starting. It is against my rules to let any man take a slave past here, unless he can satisfy them in the office that he has a right to take him along."

The officer then passed on and left me standing upon the platform, with my anxious heart apparently palpitating in the throat. At first I scarcely knew which way to turn. But it soon occurred to me that the good God, who had been with us thus far, would not forsake us at the eleventh hour. So with renewed hope I stepped into my master's carriage, to inform him of the difficulty. I found him sitting at the farther end, quite alone. As soon as he looked up and saw me, he smiled. I also tried to wear a cheerful countenance, in order to break the shock of the sad news. I knew what made him smile. He was aware that if we were fortunate we should reach our destination at five o'clock the next morning, and this made it the more painful to communicate what the officer had said; but, as there was no time to lose, I went up to him and asked him how he felt. He said, "Much better," and that he thanked God we were getting on so nicely. I then said we were not getting on quite so well as we had anticipated. He anxiously and quickly asked what was the matter. I told him. He started as if struck by lightning, and exclaimed, "Good Heavens! William, is it possible that we are, after all, doomed to hopeless bondage?" I could say nothing, my heart was too full to speak, for at first I did not know what to do. However we knew it would never do to turn back to the "City of Destruction," like Bunyan's Mistrust and Timorous, because they saw lions in the narrow way after ascending the hill Difficulty; but press on, like noble Christian and Hopeful, to the great city in which dwelt a few "shining ones."[3] So, after a few moments, I did all I could to encourage my companion, and we stepped out and made for the office: but how or where my master obtained sufficient courage to face the tyrants who had power to blast all we held dear, heaven only knows! Queen Elizabeth could not have been more terror-stricken, on being forced to land at the traitors' gate leading to the Tower, than we were on entering that office. We felt that our very existence was at stake, and that we must either sink or swim. But, as God was our present and mighty helper in this as well as in all former trials, we were able to keep our heads up and press forwards.

On entering the room we found the principal man, to whom my master said, "Do you wish to see me, sir?" "Yes," said this eagle-eyed officer; and he added, "It is against our rules, sir, to allow any person to take a slave out of Baltimore into Philadelphia, unless he can satisfy us that he has a right to take him along." "Why is that?" asked my master, with more firmness than could be expected. "Because, sir," continued he, in a voice and manner that almost chilled our blood, "if we should suffer any gentleman to take a slave past here into Philadelphia; and should the gentleman with whom the slave might be travelling turn out not to be his rightful owner, and should the proper master come and prove that his slave escaped on our road, we shall have him to pay for; and, therefore, we cannot let any slave pass here without receiving security to show, and to satisfy us, that it is all right."

This conversation attracted the attention of the large number of bustling passengers. After the officer had finished, a few of them said, "Chit, chit, chit"; not because they thought we were slaves endeavoring to escape, but merely because they thought my master was a

---

[3] Referring to John Bunyan's allegory *Pilgrim's Progress.*

slaveholder and invalid gentleman, and therefore it was wrong to detain him. The officer, observing that the passengers sympathized with my master, asked him if he was not acquainted with some gentleman in Baltimore that he could get to endorse for him, to show that I was his property, and that he had a right to take me off. He said, "No," and added, "I bought tickets in Charleston to pass us through to Philadelphia, and therefore you have no right to detain us here." "Well, sir," said the man, indignantly, "right or no right, we shan't let you go." These sharp words fell upon our anxious hearts like the crack of doom, and made us feel that hope only smiles to deceive. For a few moments perfect silence prevailed. My master looked at me, and I at him, but neither of us dared to speak a word, for fear of making some blunder that would tend to our detection. We knew that the officers had power to throw us to prison, and if they had done so we must have been detected and driven back, like the vilest felons, to a life of slavery, which we dreaded far more than sudden death.

We felt as though we had come into deep waters and were about being overwhelmed, and that the slightest mistake would clip asunder the last brittle thread of hope by which we were suspended, and let us down forever into the dark and horrible pit of misery and degradation from which we were straining every nerve to escape. While our hearts were crying lustily unto him who is ever ready and able to save, the conductor of the train that we had just left stepped in. The officer asked if we came by the train with him from Washington; he said we did, and left the room. Just then the bell rang for the train to leave, and had it been the sudden shock of an earthquake it could not have given us a greater thrill. The sound of the bell caused every eye to flash with apparent interest, and to be more steadily fixed on us than before. But, as God would have it, the officer all at once thrust his fingers through his hair, and in a state of great agitation said, "I really don't know what to do; I calculate it is all right." He then told the clerk to run and tell the conductor "let this gentleman and slave pass," adding, "As he is not well, is a pity to stop him here. We will let him go." My master thanked him, and stepped out and hobbled across the platform quickly as possible. I tumbled him unceremoniously into one of the best carriages, and leaped into mine just as the train was gliding off towards our happy destination.

* * *

We left Baltimore about eight o'clock in the evening; and not being aware of a stopping place of any consequence between there and Philadelphia, and also knowing that if we were fortunate we should be in the latter place early the next morning, I thought I might indulge in a few minutes' sleep in the car; but I, like Bunyan's Christian in the arbor, went to sleep at the wrong time, and took too long a nap. So, when the train reached Havre de Grace, all the first-class passengers had to get out of the carriages and into a ferry boat, to be ferried across the Susquehanna river, and take the train on the opposite side.

The road was constructed so as to be raised or lowered to suit the tide. So they rolled the luggage vans on to the boat, and off on the other side; and as I was in one of the apartments adjoining a baggage car, they considered it unnecessary to awaken me, and tumbled me over with the luggage. But when my master was asked to leave his seat, he found it very dark, and cold, and raining. He missed me for the first time on the journey. On all previous occasions, as soon as the train stopped, I was at hand to assist him. This caused many slaveholders to praise me very much: they said they had never before seen a slave so attentive to his master; and therefore my absence filled him with terror and confusion; the children of Israel could not have felt more troubled on arriving at the Red Sea. So he asked the conductor if he had seen anything of his slave. The man being somewhat of an abolitionist, and believing that my master was really a slaveholder, thought he would tease him a little respecting me. So he said, "No, sir; I haven't seen anything of him for some time: I have no doubt he has run away, and is in Philadelphia, free, long before now." My master knew that there was nothing in this, so he asked the conductor if he would please to see if he could find me. The man indignantly replied, "I am no slavehunter; and as far as I am concerned everybody must look after their own niggers." He went off and left the confused invalid to fancy whatever he felt inclined. My master at first thought I must have been kidnapped into slavery by someone, or left, or perhaps killed on the train. He also thought of stopping to see if he could hear anything of me, but he soon remembered that he had no money. That night all the money we had was consigned to my own pocket, because we thought, in case there were any pickpockets about, a slave's pocket would be the last one they would look for. However, hoping to meet me some day in a land of liberty, and as he had the tickets, he thought it best upon the whole to enter the boat and come off to Philadelphia, and endeavor to make his way alone in this cold and hollow world as best he could. The time was now up, so he went on board and came across with feelings that can be better imagined than described.

After the train had got fairly on the way to Philadelphia, the guard came into my car and gave me a violent shake, and bawled out at the same time, "Boy, wake up!" I started, almost frightened out of my wits. He said, "Your master is scared half to death about you." That frightened me still more—I thought they had found him out; so I anxiously inquired what was the matter. The guard said, "He thinks you have run away from him." This made me feel quite at ease. I said, "No, sir; I am satisfied my good master doesn't think that." So off I started to see him. He had been fearfully nervous, but on seeing me he at once felt much better. He merely wished to know what had become of me.

On returning to my seat, I found the conductor and two or three other persons amusing themselves very much respecting my running away. So the guard said, "Boy, what did your master want?" I replied, "He merely wished to know what had become of me." "No," said the man, "that was not it; he thought you had taken French leave, for parts unknown. I never saw a fellow so badly scared about losing his slave in my life. Now," continued the guard, "let me give you a little friendly advice. When you get to Philadelphia, run away and leave that cripple, and have your liberty." "No, sir," I indifferently replied, "I can't promise to do that." "Why not" said the conductor, evidently much surprised, "don't you want your liberty?" "Yes, sir," I replied, "but I shall never run away from such a good master as I have at present."

One of the men said to the guard, "Let him alone; I guess he will open his eyes when he gets to Philadelphia, and see things in another light." After giving me a good deal of information, which I afterwards found to be very useful, they left me alone.

I also met with a colored gentleman on this train, who recommended me to a boarding house that was kept by an abolitionist, where he thought I would be quite safe, if I wished to run away from my master. I thanked him kindly, but of course did not let him know who we were. Late at night, or rather early in the morning, I heard a fearful whistling of the steam engine; so I opened the window and looked out, and saw a large number of flickering lights in the distance, and heard a passenger in the next carriage—who also had his head out of the window—say to his companion, "Wake up, old horse, we are at Philadelphia!"

The sight of those lights and that announcement made me feel almost as happy as Bunyan's Christian must have felt when he first caught sight of the cross. I, like him, felt that the straps that bound the heavy burden to my back began to pop, and the load to roll off. I also looked, and looked again, for it appeared very wonderful to me how the mere sight of our first city of refuge should have all at once made my hitherto sad and heavy heart become so light and happy. As the train speeded on, I rejoiced and thanked God with all my heart and soul for his great kindness and tender mercy, in watching over us, and bringing us safely through.

As soon as the train had reached the platform, before it had fairly stopped, I hurried out of my carriage to my master, whom I got at once into a cab, placed the luggage on, jumped in myself, and we drove off to the boarding house which was so kindly recommended to me. On leaving the station, my master—or rather my wife, as I may now say—who had from the commencement of the journey borne up in a manner that much surprised us both, grasped me by the hand, and said, "Thank God, William, we are safe!" then burst into tears, leant upon me, and wept like a child. The reaction was fearful. So when we reached the house, she was in reality so weak and faint that she could scarcely stand alone. However, I got her into the apartments that were pointed out, and there we knelt down, on this Sabbath, and Christmas Day—a day that will ever be memorable to us—and poured out our heartfelt gratitude to God, for his goodness in enabling us to overcome so many perilous difficulties, in escaping out of the jaws of the wicked.

FREDERICK DOUGLASS AS THE BRIDGE

We have already met Frederick Douglass, who described his life in bondage in an earlier part of this book. Douglass, like the Crafts, made it safely to the northern states, traveled to England, and with the aid of Quaker abolitionists purchased his own freedom, thus protecting himself from efforts to return him to the South and slavery. He eventually became the most articulate and influential black advocate of abolition, serving as a bridge between the slave experience and the organized effort to end it. He settled finally in Rochester, New York, and there founded his newspaper, the *North Star.* We look now at three of Douglass' indictments of slavery and the nation that permitted it to flourish. The first, from his book *My Bondage and My Freedom,* describes how it felt to live freely in the North yet to be haunted by the threat of capture and the memories of enslavement:

In less than a week after leaving Baltimore, I was walking amid the hurrying throng, and gazing upon the dazzling wonders of Broadway. The dreams of my childhood and the purposes of my manhood were now fulfilled. A free state around me, and a free earth under my feet! What a moment was this to me! A whole year was pressed into a single day. A new world burst upon my agitated vision. I have often been asked, by kind friends to whom I have told my story, how I felt when first I found myself beyond the limits of slavery; and I must say here, as I have often said to them, there is scarcely anything about which I could not give a more satisfactory answer. It was a moment of joyous excitement, which no words can describe. In a letter to a friend, written soon after reaching New York, I said I felt as one might be supposed to feel, on escaping from a den of hungry lions. But, in a moment like that, sensations are too intense and too rapid for words. Anguish and grief, like darkness and rain, may be described, but joy and gladness, like the rainbow of promise, defy alike the pen and pencil.

For ten or fifteen years I had been dragging a heavy chain, with a huge block attached to it, cumbering my every motion. I had felt myself doomed to drag this chain and this block through life. All efforts, before, to separate myself from the hateful encumbrance, had only seemed to rivet me the more firmly to it. Baffled and discouraged at times, I had asked myself the question, May not this, after all, be God's work? May He not, for wise ends, have doomed me to this lot? A contest had been going on in my mind for years, between the clear consciousness of right and the plausible errors of superstition; between the wisdom of manly courage, and the foolish weakness of timidity. The contest was now ended; the chain was severed; God and right stood vindicated. I was A FREEMAN, and the voice of peace and joy thrilled my heart.

Free and joyous, however, as I was, joy was not the only sensation I experienced. It was like the quick blaze, beautiful at the first, but which subsiding, leaves the building charred and desolate. I was soon taught that I was still in an enemy's land. A sense of loneliness and insecurity oppressed me sadly. I had been but a few hours in New York, before I was met in the streets by a fugitive slave, well known to me, and the information I got from him respecting New York, did nothing to lessen my apprehension of danger. The fugitive in question was "Allender's Jake," in Baltimore; but, said he, I am "WILLIAM DIXON," in New York! I knew Jake well, and knew when Tolly Allender and Mr. Price (for the latter employed Master Hugh as his foreman, in his shipyard on Fell's Point) made an attempt to recapture Jake, and failed. Jake told me all about his circumstances, and how narrowly he escaped being taken back to slavery; that the city was now full of Southerners, returning from the springs; that the black people in New York were not to be trusted; that there were hired men on the lookout for fugitives from slavery, and who, for a few dollars, would betray me into the hands of the slave-catchers; that I must trust no man with my secret; that I must not think of going either on the wharves to work, or to a boarding-house to board; and, worse still, this same Jake told me it was not in his power to help me. He seemed, even while cautioning me, to be fearing lest, after all, I might be a party to a second attempt to recapture him. Under the inspiration of this thought, I must suppose it was, he gave signs of a wish to get rid of me, and soon left me—his whitewash brush in hand—as he said, for his work. He was soon lost to sight among the throng, and I was alone again, an easy prey to the kidnappers, if any should happen to be on my track.

New York, seventeen years ago, was less a place of safety for a runaway slave than now, and all know how unsafe it now is, under the new fugitive slave bill. I was much troubled. I had very little money—enough to buy me a few loaves of bread, but not enough to pay board, outside a lumber yard. I saw the wisdom of keeping away from the ship yards, for if Master Hugh pursued me, he would naturally expect to find me looking for work among the calkers. For a time, every door seemed closed against me. A sense of my loneliness and helplessness crept over me, and covered me with something bordering on despair. In the midst of thousands of my fellowmen, and yet a perfect stranger! In the midst of human brothers, and yet more fearful of them than of hungry wolves! I was without home, without friends, without work, without money, and without any definite knowledge of which way to go, or where to look for succor.

Some apology can easily be made for the few slaves who have, after making good their escape, turned back to slavery, preferring the actual rule of their masters, to the life of loneliness, apprehension, hunger, and anxiety, which meets them on their first arrival in a free state. It is difficult for a freeman to enter into the feelings of such fugitives. He cannot see things in the same light with the slave, because he does not, and cannot, look from the same point from which the slave does. "Why do you tremble," he says to the slave, "you are in a free state"; but the difficulty is, in realizing that he is in a free state, the slave might reply. A freeman cannot understand why the slave-master's shadow is bigger, to the slave, than the might and majesty of a free state; but when he reflects that the slave knows more about the slavery of his master than he does of the might and majesty of the free state, he has the explanation. The slave has been all his life learning the power of his master—being trained to dread his approach—and only a few hours learning the power of the state. The master is to him a stern and flinty reality, but the state is little more than a dream. He has been accustomed to regard every white man as the friend of his master, and every colored man as more or less under the control of his master's friends—the white people. It takes stout nerves to stand up, in such circumstances. A man, homeless, shelterless, breadless, friendless, and moneyless, is not in a condition to assume a very proud or joyous tone; and in just this condition was I, while wandering about the streets of New York city and lodging, at least one night, among the barrels on one of its wharves. I was not only free from slavery, but I was free from home, as well.

Next we turn to an editorial that Douglass published in his *North Star* on November 17, 1848. The newly elected president, Zachary Taylor, was a slave owner; and Douglass spoke to the nation about the evil of the condition he once shared with other black people. The editorial reads, in part, as follows:

THE BLOOD OF THE SLAVE ON THE SKIRTS OF THE NORTHERN PEOPLE

A victim of your power and oppression, humbly craves your attention to a few words, (in behalf of himself and three millions of his brethren, whom you hold in chains and slavery), with respect to the election just completed. In doing so, I desire to be regarded as addressing you, individually and collectively. If I should seem severe, remember that the iron of slavery has pierced and rankled in my heart, and that I not only smart under the recollection of a long and cruel enslavement, but am even now passing my life in a country, and among a people, whose prejudices against myself and people subjects me to a thousand poisonous stings. If I speak harshly, my excuse is, that I speak in fetters of your own forging. Remember that oppression hath the power to make even a wise man mad.

In the selection of your national rulers just completed, you have made another broad mark on the page of your nation's history, and have given to the world and the coming generation a certain test by which to determine your present integrity as a people. That actions speak louder than words—that within the character of the representative may be seen that of the constituency—that no people are better than their laws or lawmakers—that a stream cannot rise higher than its source—that a sweet fountain cannot send forth bitter water, and that a tree is to be known by its fruits, are truisms; and in their light let us examine the character and pretensions of your boasted Republic.

As a people, you claim for yourselves a higher civilization—a purer morality—a deeper religious faith—a larger love of liberty, and a broader philanthropy, than any other nation on the globe. In a word, you claim yours to be a model Republic, and promise, by the force and excellence of your institutions, and the purity and brightness of your example, to overthrow the thrones and despotisms of the old world, and substitute your own in their stead. Your missionaries are found in the remotest parts of the globe, while our land swarms with churches and religious institutions. In words of Religion and Liberty, you are abundant and preeminent. You have long desired to get rid of the odium of being regarded as pro-slavery, and have even insisted that the charge of pro-slavery made against you was a slander and that those who made it were animated by wild and fanatical spirit. To make your innocence apparent, you have now had a fair opportunity. The issue for freedom or slavery has been clearly submitted to you, and you have deliberately chosen slavery.

* * *

Do you really think to circumvent God?—Do you suppose that you can go on in your present career of injustice and political profligacy undisturbed? Has the law of righteous retribution been repealed from the statutes of the Almighty? Or what mean ye that ye bruise and bind my people? Will justice sleep forever? Oh, that you would lay these things to heart! Oh, that you would consider the enormity of your conduct, and seek forgiveness at the hands of a merciful Creator. Repent of this wickedness, and bring forth fruit meet for repentance, by delivering the despoiled out of the hands of the despoiler.

You may imagine that you have now silenced the annoying cry of abolition—that you have sealed the doom of the slave—that abolition is stabbed and dead; but you will find your mistake. You have stabbed, but the cause is not dead. Though down and bleeding at your feet, she shall rise again, and going before you, shall give you no rest till you break every yoke and let the oppressed go free. The Anti-Slavery Societies of the land will rise up and spring to action again, sending forth from the press and on the voice of the living speaker, words of burning truth, to alarm the guilty, to unmask the hypocrite, to expose the frauds of political parties, and rebuke the spirit of a corrupt and sin-sustaining church and clergy. Slavery will be attacked in its stronghold—the compromises of the Constitution, and the cry of disunion shall be more fearlessly proclaimed, till slavery be abolished, the Union dissolved, or the sun of this guilty nation must go down in blood.—F.D.

But perhaps Douglass' most powerful article, the one that still reveals most clearly his abolitionist soul, was published in William Lloyd Garrison's *Liberator* on September 22, 1848. It is an open letter to his former master Thomas Auld; and it reads, in part, as follows:

I have often thought I should like to explain to you the grounds upon which I have justified myself in running away from you. I am almost ashamed to do so now, for by this time you may have discovered them yourself. I will, however, glance at them. When yet but a child about six years old, I imbibed the determination to run away. The very first mental effort that I now remember on my part, was an attempt to solve the mystery—why am I a slave? and with this question my youthful mind was troubled for many days, pressing upon me more heavily at times than others. When I saw the slave-driver whip a slave-woman, cut the blood out of her neck, and heard her piteous cries, I went away into the corner of the fence, wept and pondered over the mystery. I had, through some medium, I know not what, got some idea of God, the Creator of all mankind, the black and the white, and that he had made the blacks to serve the whites as slaves. How he could do this and be *good,* I could not tell. I was not satisfied with this theory, which made God responsible for slavery, for it pained me greatly, and I have wept over it long and often. At one time, your first wife, Mrs. Lucretia, heard me sighing and saw me shedding tears, and asked me the matter, but I was afraid to tell her. I was puzzled with this question, till one night while sitting in the kitchen, I heard some of the old slaves talking of their parents having been stolen from Africa by white men, and were sold here as slaves. The whole mystery was solved at once. Very soon after this, my Aunt Jinny and Uncle Noah ran away, and the great noise made about it by your father-in-law, made me for the first time acquainted with the fact, that there were free states as well as slave states. From that time, I resolved that I would some day run away. The morality of the act I dispose of as follows: I am myself; you are yourself; we are two distinct persons, equal persons. What you are, I am. You are a man, and so am I. God created both, and made us separate beings. I am not by nature bound to you, or you to me. Nature does not make your existence depend upon me, or mine to depend upon yours. I cannot walk upon your legs, or you upon mine. I cannot breathe for you, or you for me; I must breathe for myself, and you for yourself. We are distinct persons, and are each equally provided with faculties necessary to our individual existence. In leaving you, I took nothing but what belonged to me, and in no way lessened your means for obtaining an *honest* living. Your faculties remained yours, and mine became useful to their rightful owner. I therefore see no wrong in any part of the transaction. It is true, I went off secretly; but that was more your fault than mine. Had I let you into the secret, you would have defeated the enterprise entirely; but for this, I should have been really glad to have made you acquainted with my intentions to leave.

You may perhaps want to know how I like my present condition. I am free to say, I greatly prefer it to that which I occupied in Maryland. I am, however, by no means prejudiced against the state as such. Its geography, climate, fertility, and products, are such as to make it a very desirable abode for any man; and but for the existence of slavery there, it is not impossible that I might again take up my abode in that state. It is not that I love Maryland less, but freedom more. You will be surprised to learn that people at the north labor under the strange delusion that if the slaves were emancipated at the south, they would flock to the north. So far from this being the case, in that event, you would see many old and familiar faces back again to the south. The fact is, there are few here who would not return to the south in the event of emancipation. We want to live in the land of our birth, and to lay our bones by the side of our fathers; and nothing short of an intense love of personal freedom keeps us from the south. For the sake of this, most of us would live, on a crust of bread and a cup of cold water.

* * *

At this moment, you are probably the guilty holder of at least three of my own dear sisters, and my only brother, in bondage. These you regard as your property. They are recorded on your ledger, or perhaps have been sold to human flesh-mongers, with a view to filling your own ever-hungry purse. Sir, I desire to know how and where these dear sisters are. Have you sold them? or are they still in your possession? What has become of them? are they living or dead? And my dear old grandmother, whom you turned out like an old horse to die in the woods—is she still alive? Write and let me know all about them. If my grandmother be still alive, she is of no service to you, for by this time she must be nearly eighty years old—too old to be cared for by one to whom she has ceased to be of service; send her to me at Rochester, or bring her to Philadelphia, and it shall be the crowning happiness of my life to take care of her in her old age. Oh! she was to me a mother and a father, so far as hard toil for my comfort could make her such. Send me my grandmother! that I may watch over and take care of her in her old age. And my sisters—let me know all about them. I would write to them, and learn all I want to know of them, without disturbing you in any way, but that, through your unrighteous conduct, they have been entirely deprived of the power to read and write. You have kept them in utter ignorance, and have therefore robbed them of the sweet enjoyments of writing or receiving letters from absent friends and relatives. Your wickedness and cruelty, committed in this respect on your fellow creatures, are greater than all the stripes you have laid upon my back or theirs. It is an outrage upon the soul, a war upon the immortal spirit, and one for which you must give account at the bar of our common Father and Creator.

The responsibility which you have assumed in this regard is truly awful, and how you could stagger under it these many years is marvelous. Your mind must have become darkened, your heart hardened, your conscience seared and petrified, or you would have long since thrown off the accursed load, and sought relief at the hands of a sin-forgiving God. How, let me ask, would you look upon me, were I, some dark night, in company with a band of hardened villains, to enter the precincts of your elegant dwelling, and seize the person of your own lovely daughter, Amanda, and carry her off from your family, friends, and all the loved ones of her youth—make her my slave—compel her to work, and I take her wages—place her name on my ledger as property—disregard her personal rights—fetter the powers of her immortal soul by denying her the right and privilege of learning to read and write—feed her coarsely—clothe her scantily, and whip her on the naked back occasionally; more, and still more horrible, leave her unprotected—a degraded victim to the brutal lust of fiendish overseers, who would pollute, blight, and blast her fair soul—rob her of all dignity—destroy her virtue, and annihilate in her person all the graces that adorn the character of virtuous womanhood? I ask, how would you regard me, if such were my conduct? Oh! the vocabulary of the damned would not afford a word sufficiently infernal to express your idea of my God-provoking wickedness. Yet, sir, your treatment of my beloved sisters is in all essential points precisely like the case I have now supposed. Damning as would be such a deed on my part, it would be no more so than that which you have committed against me and my sisters.

I will now bring this letter to a close; you shall hear from me again unless you let me hear from you. I intend to make use of you as a weapon with which to assail the system of slavery—as a means of concentrating public attention on the system, and deepening the horror of trafficking in the souls and bodies of men. I shall make use of you as a means of exposing the character of the American church and clergy—and as a means of bringing this guilty nation, with yourself, to repentance. In doing this, I entertain no malice toward you personally. There is no roof under which you would be more safe than mine, and there is nothing in my house which you might need for your comfort, which I would not readily grant. Indeed, I should esteem it a privilege to set you an example as to how mankind ought to treat each other.

> I am your fellow-man, but not your slave,
> Frederick Douglass

HARRIET BEECHER STOWE'S ELIZA

The abolitionist movement was founded by whites who sympathized with the plight of slaves and felt that the only solution to America's dilemma of slavery in a land of the free was to end the institution absolutely, finally, and immediately. Many early abolitionists were women, and almost all had strong religious convictions. One such woman, married to a theologian, was Harriet Beecher Stowe, whose brother Lyman Beecher was a prominent New York minister. To give substance to her opposition to slavery, she began publishing on June 5, 1851, a serial work of fiction called "Uncle Tom's Cabin" in a magazine called *National Era.* Her story was projected to be a short work, to run for no more than three months. On July 9, however, she wrote to Frederick Douglass, asking him for details of slave life; and thereafter the story grew. The final chapter was not published until April 1852. The following is her request to Douglass:

> Brunswick, July 9, 1851

FREDERICK DOUGLASS, ESQ.:

Sir,—You may perhaps have noticed in your editorial readings a series of articles that I am furnishing for the "Era" under the title of "Uncle Tom's Cabin, or Life among the Lowly."

In the course of my story the scene will fall upon a cotton plantation. I am very desirous, therefore, to gain information from one who has been an actual laborer on one, and it occurred to me that in the circle of your acquaintance there might be one who would be able to communicate to me some such information as I desire. I have before me an able paper written by a Southern planter, in which the details and *modus operandi* are given from his point of sight. I am anxious to have something more from another standpoint. I wish to be able to make a picture that shall be graphic and true to nature in its details. Such a person as Henry Bibb, if in the country, might give me just the kind of information I desire. You may possibly know of some other person. I will subjoin to this letter a list of questions, which in that case you will do me a favor by inclosing to the individual, with the request that he will at earliest convenience answer them.

That magazine serial, "Uncle Tom's Cabin," was published in book form in 1852 and became a best-seller, with three hundred thousand copies purchased in its first year. It had a tremendous influence on American attitudes toward slavery. On May 11, 1853, Frederick Douglass wrote: ". . . look all over the North; look South, look at home—look abroad—look at the whole civilized world—and what are all this vast multitude doing at the moment? Why sir, they are reading *Uncle Tom's Cabin.*" And when Ms. Stowe met President Lincoln he reportedly referred to her as "the little lady who started the big war." With her novel Harriet Beecher Stowe made a monumental contribution to the growing movement to abolish slavery. In the selection that follows, Stowe describes to her huge audience how a slave named Eliza started a journey to freedom, from Kentucky across the great river to Ohio. Eliza is a new mother, and she wants her child to be free, so she follows in the footsteps of Frederick Douglass, continuing to cry freedom, as did Nat Turner before her:

It is impossible to conceive of a human creature more wholly desolate and forlorn than Eliza, when she turned her footsteps from Uncle Tom's cabin.

Her husband's suffering and dangers, and the danger of her child, all blended in her mind, with a confused and stunning sense of the risk she was running, in leaving the only home she had ever known, and cutting loose from the protection of a friend whom she loved and revered. Then there was the parting from every familiar object,—the place where she had grown up, the trees under which she had played, the groves where she had walked many an evening in happier days, by the side of her young husband,—everything, as it lay in the clear, frosty starlight, seemed to speak reproachfully to her, and ask her whither could she go from a home like that?

But stronger than all was maternal love, wrought into a paroxysm of frenzy by the near approach of a fearful danger. Her boy was old enough to have walked by her side, and, in an indifferent case, she would only have led him by the hand; but now the bare thought of putting him out of her arms made her shudder, and she strained him to her bosom with a convulsive grasp, as she went rapidly forward.

The frosty ground creaked beneath her feet, and she trembled at the sound; every quaking leaf and fluttering shadow send the blood backward to her heart, and quickened her footsteps. She wondered within herself at the strength that seemed to be come upon her; for she felt the weight of her boy as if it had been a feather, and every flutter of fear seemed to increase the supernatural power that bore her on, while from her pale lips burst forth, in frequent ejaculations, the prayer to a Friend above—"Lord, help! Lord, save me!"

If it were *your* Harry, mother, or your Willie, that were going to be torn from you by a brutal trader, to-morrow morning,—if you had seen the man, and heard that the papers were signed and delivered, and you had only from twelve o'clock till morning to make good your escape,— how fast could *you* walk? How many miles could you make in those few brief hours, with the darling at your bosom,—the little sleepy head on your shoulder,—the small, soft arms trustingly holding on to your neck?

For the child slept. At first, the novelty and alarm kept him waking; but his mother so hurriedly repressed every breath or sound, and so assured him that if he were only still she would certainly save him, that he clung quietly round her neck, only asking, as he found himself sinking to sleep,

"Mother, I don't need to keep awake, do I?"

"No, my darling; sleep, if you want to."

"But, mother, if I do get asleep, you won't let him get me?"

"No! so may God help me!" said his mother, with a paler cheek, and a brighter light in her large dark eyes.

"You're *sure,* an't you mother?"

"Yes, *sure!*" said the mother, in a voice that started herself; for it seemed to her to come from a spirit within, that was no part of her; and the boy dropped his little weary head on her shoulder, and was soon asleep. How the touch of those warm arms, the gentle breathings that came in her neck, seemed to add fire and spirit to her movements! It seemed to her as if strength poured into her in electric streams, from every gentle touch and movement of the sleeping, confiding child. Sublime is the dominion of the mind over the body, that, for a time, can make flesh and nerve impregnable and string the sinews like steel, so that the weak become so mighty.

The boundaries of the farm, the grove, the wood-lot passed by her dizzily, as she walked on; and still she went, leaving one familiar object after another, slacking not, pausing not, till reddening daylight found her many a long mile from all traces of any familiar objects upon the open highway.

She had often been, with her mistress, to visit some connections, in the little village of T——, not far from the Ohio river, and knew the road well. To go thither, to escape across the Ohio river, were the first hurried outlines of her plan of escape; beyond that, she could only hope in God.

When horses and vehicles began to move along the highway, with that alert perception peculiar to a state of excitement, and which seems to be a sort of inspiration, she became aware that her headlong pace and distracted air might bring on her remark and suspicion. She therefore put the boy on the ground, and, adjusting her dress and bonnet, she walked on at as rapid a pace as she thought consistent with the preservation of appearances. In her little bundle she had provided a store of cakes and apples, which she used as expedients for quickening the speed of the child, rolling the apple some yards before them, when the boy would run with all his might after it; and this ruse, often repeated, carried them over many a half-mile.

After a while, they came to a thick patch of woodland, through which murmered a clear brook. As the child complained of hunger and thirst, she climbed over the fence with him; and, sitting down behind a large rock which concealed them from the road, she gave him a breakfast out of her little package. The boy wondered and grieved that she could not eat; and when, putting his arms round her neck, he tried to wedge some of his cake into her mouth, it seemed to her that the rising in her throat would choke her.

"No, no, Harry darling! mother can't eat till you are safe! We must go on—on—till we come to the river!" And she hurried again into the road, and again constrained herself to walk regularly and composedly forward.

She was many miles past any neighborhood where she was personally known. If she would chance to meet any who knew her, she reflected that the well-known kindness of the family would be of itself a blind to suspicion, as making it an unlikely supposition that she could be fugitive. As she was also so white as not to be known as of colored lineage, without a critical survey, and her child was white also, it was much easier for her to pass on unsuspected.

On this presumption, she stopped at noon at a neat farmhouse, to rest herself, and buy some dinner for her child and self; for, as the danger decreased with the distance, the supernatural tension of the nervous system lessened, and she found herself both weary and hungry.

The good woman, kindly and gossiping, seemed rather pleased than otherwise with having somebody come in to talk with; and accepted, without examination, Eliza's statement, that she "was going on a little piece, to spend a week with her friends,"—all of which she hoped in her heart might prove strictly true.

An hour before sunset, she entered the village of T——, by the Ohio river, weary and foot-sore, but still strong in heart. Her first glance was at the river, which lay, like Jordan, between her and the Canaan of liberty on the other side.

It was now early spring, and the river was swollen and turbulent; great cakes of floating ice were swinging heavily to and from in the turbid waters. Owing to the peculiar form of the shore on the Kentucky side, the land bending far out into the water, the ice had been lodged and detained in great quantities, and the narrow channel which swept round the bend was full of ice, piled one cake over another, thus forming a temporary barrier to the descending ice, which lodged, and formed a great undulating raft, filling up the whole river, and extending almost to the Kentucky shore.

Eliza stood, for a moment contemplating this unfavorable aspect of things, which she saw at once must prevent the usual ferry-boat from running, and then turned into a small public house on the bank, to make a few inquiries.

The hostess, who was busy in various fizzing and stewing operations over the fire, preparatory to the evening meal, stopped, with a fork in her hand, as Eliza's sweet and plaintive voice arrested her.

"What is it?" she said.

"Isn't there any ferry or boat, that takes people over to B——, now?" she said.

"No, indeed!" said the woman; "the boats has stopped running."

Eliza's look of dismay and disappointment struck the woman, and she said, inquiringly,

"May be you're wanting to get over?—anybody sick? Ye seem mighty anxious?"

"I've got a child that's very dangerous," said Eliza. "I never heard of it till last night, and I've walked quite a piece to-day, in hopes to get to the ferry."

"Well, now, that's onlucky," said the woman, whose motherly sympathies were much aroused; "I'm re'lly consarned for ye. Solomon!" she called, from the window, towards a small back building. A man, in leather apron and very dirty hands, appeared at the door.

"I say, Sol," said the woman, "is that ar man going to tote them bar'ls over to-night?"

"He said he should try, if 't was any way prudent," said the man.

"There's a man a piece down here, that's going over with some truck this evening, if he durs' to; he'll be in here to supper to-night, so you'd better set down and wait. That's a sweet little fellow," added the woman, offering him a cake.

But the child, wholly exhausted, cried with weariness.

"Poor fellow! he isn't used to walking, and I've hurried him on so," said Eliza.

"Well, take him into this room," said the woman, opening into a small bed-room, where stood a comfortable bed. Eliza laid the weary boy upon it, and held his hands in hers till he was fast asleep. For her there was no rest. As a fire in her bones, the thought of the pursuer urged her on; and she gazed with longing eyes on the sullen, surging waters that lay between her and liberty.

As she seeks to escape, Eliza is pursued by the slaveowner Haley and two of his male slaves, Sam and Andy, who are ambivalent at best about their mission.

It was about three-quarters of an hour after Eliza had laid her child to sleep in the village tavern that the party came riding into the same place. Eliza was standing by the window, looking out in another direction, when Sam's quick eye caught a glimpse of her. Haley and Andy were two yards behind. At this crisis, Sam contrived to have his hat blown off, and uttered a loud and characteristic ejaculation, which startled her at once; she drew suddenly back; the whole train swept by the window, round to the front door.

A thousand lives seemed to be concentrated in that one moment to Eliza. Her room opened by a side door to the river. She caught her child, and sprang down the steps towards it. The trader caught a full glimpse of her, just as she was disappearing down the bank; and throwing himself from his horse, and calling loudly on Sam and Andy, he was after her like a hound after a deer. In that dizzy moment her feet to her scarce seemed to touch the ground, and a moment brought her to the water's edge. Right on behind they came; and, nerved with strength such as God gives only to the desperate, with one wild cry and flying leap, she vaulted sheer over the turbid current by the shore, and on to the raft of ice beyond. It was a desperate leap—impossible to anything but madness and despair; and Haley, Sam, and Andy, instinctively cried out, and lifted up their hands, as she did it.

The huge green fragment of ice on which she alighted pitched and creaked as her weight came on it, but she staid there not a moment.

With wild cries and desperate energy she leaped to another and still another cake;—stumbling—leaping—slipping—springing upwards again! Her shoes are gone—her stockings cut from her feet—while blood marked every step; but she saw nothing, felt nothing, till dimly, as in a dream, she saw the Ohio side, and a man helping her up the bank.

"Yer a brave gal, now, whoever ye ar!" said the man, with an oath.

Eliza recognized the voice and face of a man who owned a farm not far from her old home.

"O, Mr. Symmes!—save me—do save me—do hide me!" said Eliza.

"Why, what's this?" said the man. "Why, if 'tan't Shelby's gal!"

"My child!—this boy!—he'd sold him! There is his Mas'r," said she, pointing to the Kentucky shore. "O, Mr. Symmes, you've got a little boy!"

"So I have," said the man, as he roughly, but kindly, drew her up the steep bank. "Besides, you're a right brave gal. I like grit, wherever I see it."

When they had gained the top of the bank, the man paused.

"I'd be glad to do something for ye," said he; "but then there's nowhar I could take ye. The best I can do is tell ye to go *thar*," said he, pointing to a large white house which stood by itself, off the main street of the village "Go thar; they're kind folks. Thar's no kind o' danger but they'll help you,—they're up to all that sort o' thing."

"The Lord bless you!" said Eliza, earnestly.

"No 'casion, no 'casion in the world," said the man. "what I've done's of no 'count."

"And, oh, surely, sir, you won't tell any one!"

"Go to thunder, gal! What do you take a feller for? In course not," said the man. "Come, now, go along like a likely, sensible gal, as you are. You've arnt your liberty, and you shall have it, for all me."

The woman folded her child to her bosom, and walked firmly and swiftly away. The man stood and looked after her.

"Shelby, now, mebee won't think this yer the most neighborly thing in the world; but what's a feller to do? If he catches one of my gals in the same fix, he's welcome to pay back. Somehow I never could see no kind o' critter a strivin' and pantin', and trying to clar theirselves, with the dogs arter 'em, and go agin 'em. Besides, I don't see no kind of 'casion for me to be hunter and catcher for other folks, neither."

So spoke this poor, heathenish Kentuckian, who had not been instructed in his constitutional relations, and consequently was betrayed into acting in a sort of Christianized manner, which, if he had been better situated and more enlightened, he would not have been left to do.

Haley had stood a perfectly amazed spectator of the scene, till Eliza had disappeared up the bank, when he turned a blank, inquiring look on Sam and Andy.

"That ar was a tolable fair stroke of business," said Sam.

"The gal's got seven devils in her, I believe!" said Haley. "How like a wildcat she jumped!"

"Wal, now," said Sam, scratching his head, "I hope Mas'r'll 'scuse us tryin' dat ar road. Don't think I feel spry enough for dat ar, no way!" and Sam gave a hoarse chuckle.

"*You* laugh!" said the trader, with a growl.

"Lord bless you, Mas'r, I couldn't help it, now," said Sam, giving way to the long pent-up delight of his soul. "She looked so curi's, a leapin' and springin'—ice a crackin'—and only to hear her,—plump! ker chunk! ker splash! Spring! Lord! How she goes it!" and Sam and Andy laughed till the tears rolled down their cheeks.

"I'll make ye laugh t' other side yer mouths!" said the trader, laying about their heads with his riding-whip.

Both ducked, and ran shouting up the bank, and were on their horses before he was up.

"Good-evening, Mas'r!" said Sam, with much gravity. "I berry much 'spect Missis be anxious 'bout Jerry. Mas'r Haley won't want us no longer. Missis wouldn't hear of our ridin' the critters over Lizy's bridge to-night"; and, with a facetious poke into Andy's ribs, he started off, followed by the latter, at full speed,—their shouts of laughter coming faintly on the wind.

QUESTIONS FOR RESPONSIVE ESSAYS

1. What skills did a slave need to make a successful escape from bondage? What variety of skills did the Crafts display? How might these skills have been learned despite or perhaps because of the slave experience? How might slaves have failed to escape without such skills? What unforeseen obstacles might have thwarted their escape?

2. What, according to the testimony of Frederick Douglass, were the pitfalls of freedom? What dangers lay ahead even for the slaves who escaped, even for those who were legally free? If, as Douglass believed, total abolition was the only solution to the evil of

slavery, how could abolition be achieved? What were his frustrations with his country and its government?

3. Show what Frederick Douglass and Harriet Beecher Stowe each contributed to the abolitionist cause. Show how their different achievements were affected by the differences in their color and gender. What did each one achieve that the other could not have?

PART V

Nat Turner in History

Nat Turner, both the man and the symbol, the person who led the most dramatic uprising against slavery, continued to exert a strong influence on the American Mind throughout the century after his death. His influence, almost the outline of his face, may be seen in the flight of the Crafts, the abolitionist work of Frederick Douglass, even the escape of Harriet Beecher Stowe's Eliza, but most clearly in the plot of John Brown. Slave owners and abolitionists alike continued to debate Turner's uprising in the years leading up to the Civil War, at the turn of the new century, and as long as a century after his cry for freedom in 1831.

THOMAS WENTWORTH HIGGINSON: 1861

Nat Turner was especially on American's minds after John Brown led his attack on the U.S. Army arsenal at Harpers Ferry in 1859. Brown, a white abolitionist, hoped to seize rifles, arm slaves, and send them out into the South to free their brothers. In a certain sense, Brown was a white Nat Turner. His uprising, reminiscent of

Turner's in the same state of Virginia twenty-eight years before, was a hot topic during the presidential election of 1860 and during the following year as the Civil War began. In August 1861 an article about Nat Turner, appropriate for the times, appeared in *Atlantic Monthly* magazine, written by Thomas Wentworth Higginson, a Boston abolitionist. Although he was white, Higginson later led an all-black battalion into the war and died with his men. One hundred and thirty years later he was the subject of a major motion picture entitled *Glory*. The following are his thoughts about the man who had by 1861 made an indelible impression on the American Mind:

Near the south-eastern border of Virginia, in Southampton County, there is a neighborhood known as "The Cross Keys." It lies fifteen miles from Jerusalem, the county-town, or "court-house," seventy miles from Norfolk, and about as far from Richmond. It is some ten or fifteen miles from Murfreesborough in North Carolina, and about twenty-five from the Great Dismal swamp. Up to Sunday, the 21st of August, 1831, there was nothing to distinguish it from any other rural, lethargic, slipshod Virginia neighborhood, with the due allotment of mansion-houses and log huts, tobacco-fields and "old-fields," horses, dogs, negroes, "poor white folks," so called, and other white folks, poor without being called so. One of these last was Joseph Travis, who had recently married the widow of one Putnam Moore, and had unfortunately wedded to himself her negroes also.

In the woods on the plantation of Joseph Travis, upon the Sunday just named, six slaves met at noon for what is called in the Northern States a picnic, and in the Southern a barbecue. The bill of fare was to be simple: one brought a pig, and another some brandy, giving to the meeting an aspect so cheaply convivial that no one would have imagined it to be the final consummation of a conspiracy which had been for six months in preparation. In this plot four of the men had been already initiated—Henry, Hark or Hercules, Nelson, and Sam. Two others were novices, Will and Jack by name. The party had remained together from twelve to three o'clock, when a seventh man joined them,—a short, stout, powerfully built person, of dark mulatto complexion, and strongly marked African features, but with a face full of expression and resolution. This was Nat Turner.

He was at this time nearly thirty-one years old, having been born on the 2d of October, 1800. He had belonged originally to Benjamin Turner,—from whom he took his last name, slaves having usually no patronymic;—had then been transferred to Putnam Moore, and then to his present owner. He had, by his own account, felt himself singled out from childhood for some great work; and he had some peculiar marks on his person, which, joined to his mental precocity, were enough to occasion, among his youthful companions, a superstitious faith in his gifts and destiny. He had some mechanical ingenuity also; experimentalized very early in making paper, gunpowder, pottery, and in other arts, which, in later life, he was found thoroughly to understand. His moral faculties appeared strong, so that white witnesses admitted that he had never been known to swear an oath, to drink a drop of spirits, or to commit a theft. And, in general, so marked were his early peculiarities that people said "he had too much sense to be raised; and, if he was, he would never be of any use as a slave." This impression of personal destiny grew with his growth: he fasted, prayed, preached, read the Bible, heard voices when he walked behind his plough, and communicated his revelations to the awe-struck slaves. They told him, in return, that, "if they had his sense, they would not serve any master in the world."

The biographies of slaves can hardly be individualized; they belong to the class. We know bare facts; it is only the general experience of human beings in like condition which can clothe them with life. The outlines are certain, the details are inferential. Thus, for instance, we know that Nat Turner's young wife was a slave; we know that she belonged to a different master from himself; we know little more than this, but this is much. For this is equivalent to saying, that, by day or by night, her husband had no more power to protect her than the man who lies beyond upon a plundered vessel's deck has power to protect his wife on board the pirate schooner disappearing in the horizon. She may be well treated, she may be outraged; it is in the powerlessness that the agony lies. There is, indeed, one thing more which we do know of this young woman: the Virginia newspapers state that she was tortured under the lash, after her husband's execution, to make her produce his papers: this is all.

What his private experiences and special privileges or wrongs may have been, it is therefore now impossible to say. Travis was declared to be "more humane and fatherly to his slaves than any man in the county"; but it is astonishing how often this phenomenon occurs in the contemporary annals of slave insurrections. The chairman of the county court also stated, in pronouncing sentence, that Nat Turner had spoken of his master as "only too indulgent"; but this, for some reason, does not appear in his printed Confession, which only says, "He was a kind master, and placed the greatest confidence in me." It is very possible that it may have been so, but the printed accounts of Nat Turner's person look suspicious: he is described in Gov. Floyd's proclamation as having a scar on one of his temples, also one on the back of his neck, and a large knot on one of the bones of his right arm, produced by a blow; and although these were explained away in Virginia newspapers as having been produced by fights with his companions, yet such affrays are entirely foreign to the admitted habits of the man. It must therefore remain an open question, whether the scars and the knot were produced by black hands or by white.

Whatever Nat Turner's experiences of slavery might have been, it is certain that his plans were not suddenly adopted, but that he had brooded over them for years. To this day there are traditions among the Virginia slaves of the keen devices of "Prophet Nat." If he was caught with lime and lampblack in hand, conning over a half-finished county-map on the barn-door, he was always "planning what to do if he were blind"; or, "studying how to get to Mr. Francis' house." When he had called a meeting of slaves, and some poor whites came eavesdropping, the poor whites at once became the subjects for discussion: he incidentally mentioned that the masters had been heard threatening to drive them away; one slave had been ordered to shoot Mr. Jones' pigs, another to tear down Mr. Johnson's fences. The poor whites, Johnson and Jones, ran home to see to their homesteads, and were better friends than ever to Prophet Nat. . . .

When he came, therefore, to the barbecue on the appointed Sunday, and found not these four only, but two others, his first question to the intruders was, how they came thither. To this Will answered manfully, that his life was worth no more than the others, and "his liberty was as dear to him." This admitted him to confidence; and as Jack was known to be entirely under Hark's influence, the strangers were no bar to their discussion. Eleven hours they remained there, in anxious consultation: one can imagine those dusky faces, beneath the funereal woods, and amid the flickering of pine-knot torches, preparing that stern revenge whose shuddering echoes should ring through the land so long. Two things were at last decided: to begin their work that night; and to begin it with a massacre so swift and irresistible as to create in a few days more terror than many battles, and so spare the need of future bloodshed. "It was agreed that we should commence at home on that night, and, until we had armed and equipped ourselves and gained sufficient force, neither age nor sex was to be spared: which was invariably adhered to."

John Brown invaded Virginia with nineteen men, and with the avowed resolution to take no life but in self-defence. Nat Turner attacked Virginia from within, with six men, and with the determination to spare no life until his power was established. John Brown intended to pass rapidly through Virginia, and then retreat to the mountains. Nat Turner intended to "conquer Southampton County as the white men did in the Revolution, and then retreat, if necessary, to the Dismal Swamp." Each plan was deliberately matured; each was in its way practicable; but each was defeated by a single false step, as will soon appear.

We must pass over the details of horror, as they occurred during the next twenty-four hours. Swift and stealthy as Indians, the black men passed from house to house,—not pausing, not hesitating, as their terrible work went on. In one thing they were humaner than Indians, or than white men fighting against Indians: there was no gratuitous outrage beyond the death-blow itself, no insult, no mutilation; but in every house they entered, that blow fell on man, woman, and child,—nothing that had a white skin was spared. From every house they took arms and ammunition, and from a few money. On every plantation they found recruits: those dusky slaves, so obsequious to their master the day before, so prompt to sing and dance before his Northern visitors, were all swift to transform themselves into fiends of retribution now; show them sword or musket, and they grasped it, though it were an heirloom from Washington himself. The troop increased from house to house,—first to fifteen, then to forty, then to sixty. Some were armed with muskets, some with axes, some with scythes, some came on their masters' horses. As the numbers increased, they could be divided, and the awful work was carried on more rapidly still. The plan then was for an advanced guard of horsemen to approach each house at a gallop, and surround it till the others came up. Meanwhile, what agonies of terror must have taken place within, shared alike by innocent and by guilty! what memories of wrongs inflicted on those dusky creatures, by some,—what innocent participation, by others, in the penance! The outbreak lasted for but forty-eight hours; but, during that period, fifty-five whites were slain, without the loss of a single slave. . . .

When the number of adherents had increased to fifty or sixty, Nat Turner judged it time to strike at the county-seat, Jerusalem. Thither a few white fugitives had already fled, and couriers might thence be dispatched for aid to Richmond and Petersburg, unless promptly intercepted. Besides, he could there find arms, ammunition, and money; though they had already obtained, it is dubiously reported, from eight hundred to one thousand dollars. On the way it was necessary to pass the plantation of Mr. Parker, three miles from Jerusalem. Some of the men wished to stop here and enlist some of their friends. Nat Turner objected, as the delay might prove danger-ous; he yielded at last, and it proved fatal.

He remained at the gate with six or eight men; thirty or forty went to the house, half a mile distant. They remained too long, and he went alone to hasten them. During his absence a party of eighteen white men came up suddenly, dispersing the small guard left at the gate; and when the main body of slaves emerged from the house, they encountered, for the first time, their armed masters. The blacks halted; the whites advanced cautiously within a hundred yards, and fired a volley; on its being returned, they broke into disorder, and hur-riedly retreated, leaving some wounded on the ground. The retreating whites were pursued, and were saved only by falling in with another band of fresh men from Jerusalem, with whose aid they turned upon the slaves, who in their turn fell into confusion. Turner, Hark, and about twenty men on horseback retreated in some order; the rest were scattered. The leader still planned to reach Jerusalem by a private way, thus evading pursuit; but at last decided to stop for the night, in the hope of enlisting additional recruits.

During the night the number increased again to forty, and they encamped on Major Ridley's plantation. An alarm took place during the darkness,—whether real or imaginary, does not appear,—and the men became scattered again. Proceeding to make fresh enlistments with the daylight, they were resisted at Dr. Blunt's house, where his slaves, under his orders, fired upon them; and this, with a later attack from a party of white men near Capt. Harris', so broke up the whole force that they never reunited. The few who remained together agreed to separate for a few hours to see if anything could be done to revive the insurrection, and meet again that evening at their original rendezvous. But they never reached it.

Gloomily came Nat Turner at nightfall into those gloomy woods where forty-eight hours before he had revealed the details of his terri-ble plot to his companions. At the outset all his plans had succeeded; every thing was as he predicted: the slaves had come readily at his call; the masters had proved perfectly defenceless. Had he not been persuaded to pause at Parker's plantation, he would have been master before now of the arms and ammunition at Jerusalem; and with these to aid, and the Dismal Swamp for a refuge, he might have sustained himself indefinitely against his pursuers.

Now the blood was shed, the risk was incurred, his friends were killed or captured, and all for what? lasting memories of terror, to be sure, for his oppressors; but, on the other hand, hopeless failure for the insurrection, and certain death for him. What a watch he must have kept that night! To that excited imagination, which had always seen spirits in the sky and blood-drops on the corn and hieroglyphic marks on the dry leaves, how full the lonely forest must have been of signs and solemn warnings! Alone with the fox's bark, the rabbit's rustle, and the screech-owl's scream, the self-appointed prophet brooded over his despair. Once creeping to the edge of the wood, he saw men stealthily approach on horseback. He fancied them some of his companions; but before he dared to whisper their ominous names, "Hark" or "Dred,"—for the latter was the name, since famous, of one of his more recent recruits,—he saw them to be white men, and shrank back stealthily beneath his covert.

There he waited two days and two nights,—long enough to satisfy himself that no one would rejoin him, and that the insurrection had hopelessly failed. The determined, desperate spirits who had shared his plans were scattered forever, and longer delay would be destruction for him also. He found a spot which he judged safe, dug a hole under a pile of fence-rails in a field, and lay there for six weeks, only leaving it for a few moments at midnight to obtain water from a neighboring spring. Food he had previously provided, without discovery, from a house near by.

Meanwhile an unbounded variety of rumors went flying through the State. The express which first reached the governor announced that the militia were retreating before the slaves. An express to Petersburg further fixed the number of militia at three hundred, and of blacks at eight hundred, and invented a convenient shower of rain to explain the dampened ardor of the whites. Later reports described the slaves as making three desperate attempts to cross the bridge over the Nottoway between Cross Keys and Jerusalem, and stated that the leader had been shot in the attempt. Other accounts up the number of negroes at three hundred, all well mounted and armed, with two or three white men as leaders. Their intent was supposed to be to reach the Dismal Swamp, and they must be hemmed in from that side. . . .

Meanwhile the cause of all this terror was made the object of desperate search. On Sept. 17 the governor offered a reward of five hundred dollars for his capture; and there were other rewards, swelling the amount to eleven hundred dollars,—but in vain. No one could track or trap him. On Sept. 30 a minute account of his capture appeared in the newspapers, but it was wholly false. On Oct. 7 there was another, and on Oct. 18 another; yet all without foundation. Worn out by confinement in his little cave, Nat Turner grew more adventurous, and began to move about stealthily by night, afraid to speak to any human being, but hoping to obtain some information that might aid his escape. Returning regularly to his retreat before daybreak, he might possibly have continued this mode of life until pursuit had ceased, had not a dog succeeded where men had failed. The creature accidentally smelt out the provisions hid in the cave and finally led thither his masters, two negroes, one of whom was named Nelson. On discovering the formidable fugitive, they fled precipitately, when he hastened to retreat in an opposite direction. This was on Oct. 15; and from this moment the neighborhood was all alive with excitement, and five or six hundred men undertook the pursuit.

It shows a more than Indian adroitness in Nat Turner to have escaped capture any longer. The cave, the arms, the provisions, were found; and, lying among them, the notched stick of this miserable Robinson Crusoe, marked with five weary weeks and six days. But the man was gone. For ten days more he concealed himself among the wheat-stacks on Mr. Francis' plantation, and during this time was reduced almost to despair. Once he decided to surrender himself, and walked by night within two miles of Jerusalem before his purpose failed him. Three times he tried to get out of that neighborhood, but in vain: travelling by day was of course out of the question, and by night he found it impossible to elude the patrol. Again and again, therefore, he returned to his hiding-place; and, during his whole two months' liberty, never went five miles from the Cross Keys. On the 25th of October, he was at last discovered by Mr. Francis as he was emerging from a stack. A load of buckshot was instantly discharged at him, twelve of which passed through his hat as he fell to the ground. He escaped even then; but his pursuers were rapidly concentrating upon him, and it is perfectly astonishing that he could have eluded them for five days more.

On Sunday, Oct. 30, a man named Benjamin Phipps, going out for the first time on patrol duty, was passing at noon a clearing in the woods where a number of pine-trees had long since been felled. There was a motion among their boughs; he stopped to watch it; and through a gap in the branches he saw, emerging from a hole in the earth beneath, the face of Nat Turner. Aiming his gun instantly, Phipps called on him to surrender. The fugitive, exhausted with watching and privation, entangled in the branches, armed only with a sword, had nothing to do but to yield,—sagaciously reflecting, also, as he afterwards explained, that the woods were full of armed men, and that he had better trust fortune for some later chance of escape, instead of desperately attempting it then. He was correct in the first impression, since there were fifty armed scouts within a circuit of two miles. His insurrection ended where it began; for this spot was only a mile and a half from the house of Joseph Travis.

Torn, emaciated, ragged, "a mere scarecrow," still wearing the hat perforated with buckshot, with his arms bound to his sides, he was driven before the levelled gun to the nearest house, that of a Mr. Edwards. He was confined there that night; but the news had spread so rapidly that within an hour after his arrival a hundred persons had collected, and the excitement became so intense "that it was with difficulty he could be conveyed alive to Jerusalem." The enthusiasm spread instantly through Virginia: M. Trezvant, the Jerusalem postmaster, sent notices of it far and near; and Gov. Floyd himself wrote a letter to the Richmond *Enquirer* to give official announcement of the momentous capture.

When Nat Turner was asked by Mr. T. R. Gray, the counsel assigned him, whether, although defeated, he still believed in his own Providential mission, he answered, as simply as one who came thirty years after him, "Was not Christ crucified?" In the same spirit, when arraigned before the court, "he answered, 'Not guilty,' saying to his counsel that he did not feel so." But apparently no argument was made in his favor by his counsel, nor were any witnesses called,—he being convicted on the testimony of Levi Waller, and upon his own confession, which was put in by Mr. Gray, and acknowledged by the prisoner before the six justices composing the court, as being "full, free, and voluntary." He was therefore placed in the paradoxical position of conviction by his own confession, under a plea of "Not guilty." The arrest took place on the 30th of October, 1831, the confession on the 1st of November. The trial and conviction on the 5th, and the execution on the following Friday, the 11th of November, precisely at noon. He met his death with perfect composure, declined addressing the multitude assembled, and told the sheriff in a firm voice that he was ready. Another account says that he "betrayed no emotion, and even hurried the executioner in the performance of his duty." "Not a limb nor a muscle was observed to move. His body, after his death, was given over to the surgeons for dissection."

The confession of the captive was published under authority of Mr. Gray, in a pamphlet, at Baltimore. Fifty thousand copies of it are said to have been printed; and it was "embellished with an accurate likeness of the brigand, taken by Mr. John Crawley, portrait-painter, and lithographed by Endicott & Swett, at Baltimore." The newly established *Liberator* said of it, at the time, that it would "only serve to rouse up other leaders, and hasten other insurrections," and advised grand juries to indict Mr. Gray. I have never seen a copy of the original pamphlet; it is not easily to be found in any of our public libraries; and I have heard of but one as still existing, although the Confession itself has been repeatedly reprinted. Another small pamphlet, containing the main features of the outbreak, was published at New York during the same year, and this is in my possession. But the greater part of the facts which I have given were gleaned from the contemporary newspapers.

Who now shall go back thirty years, and read the heart of this extraordinary man, who, by the admission of his captors, "never was known to swear an oath, or drink a drop of spirits"; who, on the same authority, "for natural intelligence and quickness of apprehension was surpassed by few men," "with a mind capable of attaining any thing"; who knew no book but his Bible, and that by heart; who devoted himself soul and body to the cause of his race, without a trace of personal hope or fear; who laid his plans so shrewdly that they came at last with less warning than any earthquake on the doomed community around; and who, when that time arrived, took the life of man, woman, and child, without a throb of compunction, a word of exultation, or an act of superfluous outrage? Mrs. Stowe's "Dred" seems dim and melodramatic beside the actual Nat Turner, and De Quincey's "Avenger" is his only parallel in imaginative literature. Mr. Gray, his counsel, rises into a sort of bewildered enthusiasm with the prisoner before him. "I shall not attempt to describe the effect of his narrative, as told and commented on by himself, in the condemned hole of the prison. The calm, deliberate composure with which he spoke of his late deeds and intentions, the expression of his fiend-like face when excited by enthusiasm, still bearing the stains of the blood of helpless innocence about him, clothed with rags and covered with chains, yet daring to raise his manacled hands to heaven, with a spirit soaring above the attributes of man,—I looked on him, and the blood curdled in my veins." . . .

While these things were going on, the enthusiasm for the Polish Revolution was rising to its height. The nation was ringing with a peal of joy, on hearing that at Frankfort the Poles had killed fourteen thousand Russians. The *Southern Religious Telegraph* was publishing an impassioned address to Kosciuszko; standards were being consecrated for Poland in the larger cities; heroes like Skrzynecki, Czartoryski, Riozyski, Raminiski, were choking the trump of Fame with their complicated patronymics. These are all forgotten now; and this poor negro, who did not even possess a name, beyond one abrupt monosyllable,—for even the name of Turner was the master's property,—still lives, a memory of terror, and a symbol of wild retribution.

WILLIAM S. DREWRY: 1900

American slaves were freed not—as is popularly thought—by President Lincoln's Emancipation Proclamation, but rather by the Thirteenth Amendment to the Constitution. After this amendment was passed in 1865, slavery was ended, and the system against which Nat Turner revolted lay in the past. A year later the Fourteenth Amendment gave freed slaves the civil rights of white Americans. In reality, however, most black Americans were free in name only; and during the years after the Civil War they continued to live, particularly in the South, in much the same conditions that they had known before emancipation.

Black Americans were economically dependent upon the white owners of land, and as sharecroppers who had to pay with a share of their crops for the right to farm the land, they were little better off than their slave ancestors. They were segregated from whites by black codes regarding hotels, restaurants, trains, and schools. In 1896 the U.S. Supreme Court upheld the southern system of segregation, and thus inequality, by finding that separate facilities, so long as they were "equal," were perfectly constitutional. Toward the end of the nineteenth century lynchings—public hangings of blacks by mobs without the benefit of trials for their alleged crimes—became almost commonplace. Nat Turner would have understood the new system quite well because it was not far removed from the one he had known in 1831.

In 1900 a white Virginian, William S. Drewry, wrote the first book-length study of Nat Turner. In the following excerpt, he expresses the sentiments of most white southerners of his day and interprets Nat Turner's revolt in the light of what was occurring in turn-of-the-century southern America. Needless to say, his interpretation of Nat differs from that of the abolitionist Higginson. It is more in line with that of U.B. Phillips, a historian who at this time created the myth of the happy slave:

The slaves were cared for with the greatest kindness. The white master did not treat his slave as his ox. Slavery was simply domestic servitude, under practically efficient guarantees against ill-treatment. The system was more on the order of that in the Mosaic law, where the slave was a member of the family, and to insult or maltreat a slave was an insult which had to be atoned for upon the field of honor. The slave quarters formed a long street in the rear of the dwelling of the master, resembling a medieval village community, and during the cold winter nights the last duty of the master before retiring was to visit these quarters to see that the children were well provided with food, covering, and fuel. In many respects the slave fared better than the master. There was an attachment between the blacks and whites which is difficult to describe, and which was exhibited until within a few years past, when the population of Southampton was contaminated by the influx of foreigners employed in saw mills and railroad work. Both races were benefitted and a noble people developed, the native blacks being the equals of any of their race. Gentle treatment rendered the slave not only more faithful and affectionate, but more intelligent, and his condition, in fact, approximated that of a free servant. Slaves were the happiest laboring class in the world, and under these most favorable conditions furnished a contradiction of the "orthodox" economic theory as to the unproductiveness of slave labor. The oldest inhabitants of the county state that Southampton saw its most prosperous and progressive days between 1830 and 1861, notwithstanding the fact that tobacco and cotton had declined, and the most severe panic in the history of the United states occurred in 1837 and 1841. The condition of the Southern States is much improved since 1865. This is partly the effect of the general advance of civilization, and cannot be entirely attributed to the abolition of slavery. Besides, the greatest advance is seen in the cities, while in the rural districts, where the greatest number of slaves were owned, the condition of agriculture is very little improved, and in some sections is on a decline. The system of labor seems to have been an ideal one.

* * *

Such was the state of society in which was reared Nat Turner. He was endowed with a natural intelligence and quickness possessed by few men, with a mind capable of high attainments, but warped and perverted by the influence of early as well as later impressions. His case should be an important and useful lesson in the experience of a mind like his endeavoring to grapple with things beyond its reach. He was a careful student of the Bible, a Baptist preacher, read the newspapers and every book within his reach, and listened attentively to the discussions of political and social questions by the best and most enlightened men of the country. His sphere of action was too small for such a mind, and, consequently, he deemed it possible to conquer the county, march to the Dismal Swamp, collecting the slaves as he went, and so gradually overcome the state, as the American had the British in the Revolutionary War, all to "call the attention of the civilized world to the condition of his race." After his failure he confessed that he had been mistaken in the practicability of his scheme, frustrated both by the ready assembling of the whites and the want of discipline among his men.

Cruel treatment was not a motive for the rebellion. If this had been the case, it would have been urged in mitigation of Nat's punishment. On the contrary, he stated in his testimony that he had no reason to complain of Mr. Travis, who was a kind master, and placed the greatest confidence in him. Nat was a complete fanatic, and believed the Lord had destined him to free his race. The red tint of the autumn leaves was a sign of the blood which was to be shed. And his last text at Barnes' Church, a few days before the massacre, indicates the trend of his mind. It reads: "And I saw, and behold a white horse: and he that sat on him had a bow; and a crown was given unto him: and he went forth conquering and to conquer." Though Nat was a religious fanatic, yet he deemed any means justifiable for the accomplishment of his purpose and for making the impression that he was a prophet and servant of God. He wrote hieroglyphics and quotations on leaves and blades of fodder, and these found, according to his prediction, caused the slaves to believe him a miraculous being, endowed with supernatural powers. He spat blood at pleasure, but it proved to be the coloring matter of the log-wood, stolen from his master's dye pots. At his baptism crowds gathered, some from curiosity and others from a belief in his prophecy that a white dove would descend from heaven and alight upon his shoulder. This prophecy explains the reviling to which he refers in his confession, no doubt, with the intention of making the impression that the white people disapproved of religious toleration. That Nat was believed must not be taken as proof of the ignorance and exclusive superstition of the blacks. It is the custom to consider whites as far advanced as they are at present, and the slaves as debased, ignorant, and superstitious creatures as in their native state. But the eclipse of the sun in February, and its peculiar appearance in August, 1831, had as grave an effect upon the former as upon the latter. The "green" or "blue" day is still remembered by some of our citizens, and at the time something terrible was hourly expected. Upon the scaffold Nat declared that after his execution it would grow dark and rain for the last time. It did actually rain, and there was for some time a dry spell. This alarmed many of the whites as well as the negroes. Conjuring was the Southern counterpart of the old Puritan belief in witchcraft. It is generally attributed to the negroes, some of whom professed to be "conjur doctors," but many a gouty master believed himself conjured. Nor are such signs of superstition and fear wanting at the present day. The negroes are still afraid to pass grave-yards and places where murders have been committed, and see the wrath of God in every unusual occurrence.

Thus the insurrection "was not instigated by motives of revenge or sudden anger, but the result of long deliberation and a settled purpose of mind, the offspring of gloomy fanaticism acting upon materials but too well prepared for such impressions," and love of self-importance, encouraged by the efforts of negro preachers, who were influenced by external affairs, and employed in circulating inflammatory and seditious periodicals. Those who have received most are the most jealous and ready to complain. Nat Turner, as the Southampton slaves in general, was like a spoiled child, who, having been allowed too many privileges in youth, soon thinks he ought to be master of all he surveys. The calling of a Constitutional Convention, to meet in October, 1829, inspired in the slaves of Matthews, Isle of Wight, and the neighboring counties hopes of emancipation, and in case of failure of such declaration a determination to rebel and massacre the whites. Doubtless Nat had heard the same subjects discussed, and, being conscious of the results of the convention, which not only failed to emancipate the slaves, but limited the right of suffrage to the whites, he considered it time to carry out his threats. He was undoubtedly inspired with the hope of freedom, and the mere discussion of emancipation by a convention may have led him to believe that many of the whites would sympathize with his schemes. He is said to have passed the home of some poor white people because he considered it useless to kill those who thought no better of themselves than they did of the negroes. He also said that after he had gained a firm foothold he intended to spare all the women and children and the men who offered no resistance. But the watch word of all was indiscriminate slaughter and plunder.

* * *

The Southampton insurrection was a landmark in the history of slavery. Little was known of it on account of the suppression by the Southern States of all such reports as were likely to arouse an insurrectionary spirit and because of exaggerated accounts given in the north. It was the forerunner of the great slavery debates which resulted in the abolition of slavery in the United States, and was, indirectly, most instrumental in bringing about this result. Its importance is truly conceived by the old negroes of Southampton and vicinity, who reckon all time from "Nat's Fray," or "Old Nat's War." It is, in fact, the only plot by rebellious southern negroes which deserves the name of insurrection. More negroes were connected with the Gabriel insurrection, but they were discovered, dispersed, and their leader executed without the loss of one white person. Both were influenced by the attempts of former insurgent slaves, but the Southampton rebellion was directly encouraged by the abolition movement in the United States, while Gabriel met with encouragement only from foreigners. The two insurrections also agree in that, in both, religious fanaticism and delusion played a very important role. The true character of the negro and the nature of the institution of slavery in the American colonies and States can best be learned from a thorough study of slave revolts.

* * *

History records no instance in which two races equally free have lived together in harmony. The Anglo-Boer dispute in the Transvaal is a question of race supremacy, and Sir Alfred Milner, the British Commissioner in South Africa, says: "It seems a paradox, but it is true that the only effective way of protecting our subjects is to help them to cease to be our subjects." Mr. Jefferson said that the negro and white races, equally free, could not live under the same government. They cannot amalgamate and solve the question as did Greece and Rome. Consequently, either the negro must be colonized or occupy an inferior position. But that the negroes may occupy an inferior position in the United States, they must be equally distributed in all sections of the country. Otherwise in those sections farthest removed there will exist sympathy for the negro, and a misconception and misrepresentation of the relation of the two races. The whites of the North and West believe the negro is cheated and persecuted. In many sections it is actually believed that rejected lovers in the South black themselves and commit the outrages so frequently perpetrated by negroes. So far the two races have lived in the South as equals before the law, because the majority of the negroes remain conscious of the superiority of the white race. For this reason negro labor has been preferred to white. The negro gladly accepts gifts in the form of food, old clothes, etc., and performs menial services, as cook, coachman, and servant of every description. Custom and habit exclude the poor whites of the South from such offices. In this way the negroes are rapidly acquiring property which, together with the free schools, supported principally by the whites, free amusement, and cheap newspapers, enables them to give their children educations equal to that of the ordinary whites, while the poorer whites are unable to secure even common-school education. Consequently, the number of servants in the South is gradually decreasing, and the

white people learning to perform for themselves the ordinary services. But this education of the negro, which fits him for the highest
offices in the land, renders him a useless and discontented citizen.
The whites cannot submit to negro rule and self-assertion. With the
negroes equally distributed over the Union, this could be easily
avoided. But so long as they remain with equal citizenship in the
South they will continue a burden to themselves and to the white
population. The South will remain the "Solid South" and prefer exclu-
sion from national offices rather than allow the State offices to fall
into the hands of negroes.

RAYFORD LOGAN: 1931

For black Americans, however, Nat Turner was not the enigma that
he seems to have been for whites. Black Americans understood the
sorrows that their people had known in bondage. They understood
quite well why he had sacrificed so many lives, including his own,
for his cry of freedom. Living through the dark days of oppression
that followed legal emancipation, the economic and social tyranny
of the continuing white power structure, they saw Nat Turner as a
freedom fighter, an example for their own day. To demonstrate the
image of Nat among the black population we turn to an interpretive
historical sketch by Rayford Logan, written in 1931 at the centennial
of Nat's uprising and published in *Opportunity*, a publication of the
Urban League, an organization dedicated to the advancement of
black people, particularly in urban areas. Logan begins with a description of the way slaves were brought to the New World and then
ties that history to Nat Turner:

The slaves "were tied to pole in rows, four feet apart; loose wicker
bandage around the neck of each, connected him to the pole, and the
arms being pinioned by a bandage affixed behind above the elbows,
they had sufficient room to feed, but not to loose themselves. . . .
Often did they look back with tears in their eyes." Some went mad
and laughed back at the hyenas. Some died under the lash. Others
sought certain death through flight or mutiny. Still others refused to
die before they had a chance to kill.

Death marched with the Black Ivory—but would it be always to
the black man to whom it beckoned?

Death reaped another black harvest in the barracoons and during
the embarkation. Some slaves preferred the shark's belly to the

journey beyond the seas. Death revelled in the vile ship's hold amid the offal of those dying with dysentery and groaned with those going blind from ophthalmia. It led the slaves to promise not to throw themselves overboard if given a breath of air on deck. They promised—and threw themselves to the sharks.

A ship hails in sight. Is it rescuer or kidnaper? Their ship, every sail gasping for wind, runs away. The sea is becalmed; their pursuer closes. The captain manacles the slaves to the anchor chain on the far side of the ship. Just before the English officers come on board, he cuts the chain and six hundred men, women, and children go to Davey Jones' locker. The captain is not arrested, because there is no "evidence." He returns to Africa and a thousand more children are left orphans, a dozen more wenches are chosen to grace the sailors' bed, and a thousand more men die so that five hundred or four hundred or one hundred may till the fields of the Land of the Free.

* * *

For two centuries the gentle souls of the Western Hemisphere lolled at their ease on their plantations, their *habitations,* and their *haciendas* while fifty million corpses were rotting in Africa, the depths of the seas, and on the coasts of the western world. The fate of the living was sometimes worse: husband was torn from wife and mother from child. And yet they sang. They had to sing or die or kill.

On August 21, 1831 Nat Turner, a deeply religious, highly moral Negro slave belonging to one Travis of Southampton County, Virginia, stopped singing and praying and led an insurrection in which fifty-five white men, women, and children were killed. One white for each million Africans. Nat was a long way from a reckoning either according to Bible or the Constitution of the United States which rated five Negroes equal to three white men.

So long as Nat was at large, Virginia shuddered. A thousand troops could not find him. The imagination of the planters heard bare feet gliding on the roof when the autumn leaves fell. In the twilight it saw bully black forms assemble silently behind ghostlike trees. The sighing winds brought chants from Dismal Swamp where the murderers were whetting their axes. From North Carolina came rumors of "Walarums and excursions." The *Macon Messenger* barely got off the press because all the able-bodied men were on patrol. New Orleans trembled at the report that a black man had twelve hundred stand of arms in his cellar. "Pity us!" implored a correspondent from Kentucky. The South was scared—scared as it perhaps never was before or since. The least frightened denied Divine Retribution.

Such terror demanded relief. Since Nat could not be found, any "nigger" would do. One man admitted killing ten or fifteen. General Eppes, commanding the troops, officially denounced the "revolting, inhuman, acts of barbarity." The slaughter continued. At the same time Virginia was praying, for further success to the Poles who were reported as having butchered 14,000 Russians.

The coincidences of history afford alluring speculation. November eleventh is now an occasion for rejoicing at the conclusion, stupefaction at the beginning, of the greatest holocaust of the modern age, and preparation for the next. To 12,000,000 black folk it should be a day of pride—for on that day one hundred years ago a black man kept his "Rendezvous with Death" rather than live a bondsman. His simple courage surpassed the comprehension of his executioners as did that of the Man of Galilee.

There are those who would have you believe that Nat Turner's insurrection was a failure. It is true that his executioners divided his remains for souvenirs, thus setting perhaps a precedent for a later American outdoor sport. The punishment meted out to him and to his accomplices effectively discouraged any other insurrections of note. The board of education of a Virginia county recently denied a petition for a colored training school because of the execrable memory of Nat Turner. No monument commemorates his deed. And in 1930 a Negro college professor told a white audience that the Negro will probably be back in captivity in the next twenty-five years.

But did he die in vain? By a peculiar and unwitting coincidence the lock and key of the jail in which Nat was confined lie in a case in the Virginia State Library next to the call to arms issued in Lexington County, Virginia, at the outbreak of the Civil War. No one would be foolhardy enough to assert that Nat Turner's Insurrection caused the Civil War. One may safely declare, however, that it did reveal the only solution to America's Gordian knot—the sword. Slavery had rung again as "an alarum bell in the night," and some already realized that the "panacea of palaver" was as worthless as all other nostrums.

At first the South sought to repress any other attempts to gain freedom by force. Systematic conversions to the Christian Church taught the proper submission. Dialecticians proved that converting a slave did not make him free. The most rigorous and drastic regulations were enacted to prevent any recurrence of insurrections.

The planters blamed Garrison and his *Liberator* for the insurrection. This accusation is probably unfounded, but who will deny that Nat's effort crystallized the fighting ideals of the Abolitionists? Let him who would be free strike the first blow. Lovejoy[4] and John Brown would not have been ashamed to be called the spiritual descendants of this black slave. Wendell Phillips in eulogizing Toussaint Louverture must have seen in him a kindred spirit. Even the Quakers, who suffered ostracism and imprisonment for their underground activities, must have gained respect for a race that produced men who preferred death to slavery.

And finally, the South erected a gigantic defense mechanism to justify their "peculiar institution." Only savages, they shouted, would revolt against such an idyllic state as slavery. The slave was better off than he would have been in Africa. Had he not come to know the Anglo-Saxon God, and, hence, gained a passport to Heaven? His fate was better than that of white laborers in the North or in Europe, than that of free Negroes. He was sure of his job, was he not? Black mammies, although not allowed to keep their own children, had the privilege and honor of allowing the best blood of the South to suckle at their breasts. Some white men held black wenches in such high esteem that they used them to increase their human stock exactly as they used studs to increase their stables. Though slaves, they were erecting a Kingdom of Cotton that all of Europe would not dare attack. They made possible as fine a breed of gentlemen as ever knew how to ride to hounds, drink mint juleps, betray their wives, turn a "bon mot," dance the reel, carve a wild boar, and amass debts that they could not pay. Had the Roman latifundia or the *haciendas* of New Spain created anything finer? Why in the name of an Almighty and just God should these beasts want to kill fifty men, women, and children?

The dead tell no tales, not even fifty million of them.

No reputable historian doubts that the period from 1831 to 1861 was the most horrible era of slavery. As the abolitionists redoubled their attacks the South increased its drastic regulations and pious preachments. Driven from post to post, the planters finally proclaimed slavery such a fine thing that it could not, by the laws of man or the will of God, be kept out of the newly acquired federal territory, out of the Caribbean, out of the old Northwest Territory, out of the free states themselves. In 1860 a man practically unknown but destined to become the Greatest American, peculiarly ugly but performing perhaps the only true "beau geste" in American history, was

---

[4] Elijah P. Lovejoy was an abolitionist newspaper editor who was killed by a mob at Alton, Illinois, in 1837.

elected on a platform that declared, among other things, the power of Congress to exclude slavery from federal territory. The South, proclaiming "Better out of the Union with slavery than in it without slavery," placed its trust in the arbitrament of war and the justice of God. The gallantry of the South fighting a lost cause is still the theme of poetry and history. Nat Turner, ignominiously hanged for seeking liberty, is mentioned only to be execrated as a bloodthirsty beast.

* * *

The South no longer shackles black bodies—that is, in general. It has, however, enslaved the minds of black folk just as surely as it once did their bodies. What a glorious task on this, the one-hundredth anniversary of Nat Turner's Insurrection, to dedicate ourselves to the emancipation of the minds of twelve million black folk. One may even hope for some little intelligence from the white master minds. If not, who will dare predict that there will never be another Nat Turner?

QUESTIONS FOR RESPONSIVE ESSAYS

1. How does the account of Nat Turner's revolt written by Thomas Higginson in 1861 reflect the year in which the Civil War had just begun? How does it reveal the assumptions and racial attitudes of this Boston abolitionist? What image of Nat Turner does it seek to convey, and why did Higginson believe it important to convey this image?

2. How does Wiiliam Drewry's biography of Nat Turner, written by a white southerner in 1900, reflect Drewry's day and his own assumptions? In what ways is it and is it not a true biography of Nat Turner? How does Drewry's interpretation differ from that of Higginson, and how do you account for the differences between these two white writers? Where do you hear and see their two attitudes in our own day?

3. How does the image of Nat Turner presented by Rayford Logan in 1931 agree with and differ from that of the first two writers? How does he use Nat Turner and his uprising to inspire oppressed black people a hundred years after Turner died? How does he handle the violence that is integral to Turner's story?

PART VI

William Styron's Nat Turner: An Old Controversy Renewed

American slaves may have been freed by the Thirteenth Amendment to the Constitution in 1865 and granted equality by the Fourteenth in 1866, but a century passed during which freedmen and their descendants lived in economic slavery with few civil liberties, particularly in the South. Then in the 1950s and 1960s came the civil rights movement, and for more than a decade the place and standing of black Americans were constantly in the headlines. At the height of this controversial period Nat Turner, symbol of black liberation, made a dramatic return to center stage of American history. Oddly enough, his appearance came under the direction of a white novelist from Virginia; and the highly successful fictional account of Nat's life became the focus of an intense debate, which itself helped further to mold the American Mind.

William Styron, the Virginian who wrote *The Confessions of Nat Turner* in 1966, considered himself a white liberal and believed sincerely that he had explained the nature of slavery and spoken the words of a slave to an audience that would appreciate his message of brotherhood. Yet Styron let his Nat sum up "the central madness of nigger existence" in this way: ". . . hurt a nigger, starve him, leave him wallowing . . . and he will be yours for life. Awe him by some unforeseen hint of philanthropy, tickle him with the idea of hope, and he will want to slice your throat." Styron's approach to Nat—and his shock when his approach caused such a stir—clearly reflected the attitude of many white men who considered themselves liberals in the 1960s.

THE NOVEL:
THE CONFESSIONS OF NAT TURNER

In the excerpts that follow, Styron's Nat Turner

1) recounts how it felt when he first realized that he was different from his fellow slaves;
2) feels drawn to Margaret Whitehead, a white girl who has shared her love of poetry with him; and
3) kills Margaret during the insurrection.

These three passages are chosen because they caused such controversy when the novel became a best-seller:

1.

It must have been during the spring of my sixteenth year that Marse Samuel took me aside on the lawn after one mid-day dinner and announced a rather surprising change in the routine of my life. Despite the sense I had of belonging and of a closeness to the family, I was not of course really of the family and there were intimacies I was denied; days and weeks might go by without Marse Samuel paying any note of me, especially during the long busy seasons of planting and harvest, and thus those special moments when I was the object of his attention I can recall with the greatest clearness and intensity. On this particular afternoon he spoke of my work in the house, commending me on my alertness and industry and on the good reports brought to him by Miss Nell and the young mistresses regarding the nimble way I applied myself not only to my lessons but to my daily chores.

Now, all this was laudable, he said, and the duteous way I attended to my work was something in which I myself should take pride. The fact remained, however, that I owned too much ability and intelligence to labor for long as a house servant—a career which could not help but stunt and diminish the capacities he felt I had for development and lead me early into a barren dead end. Did I not honestly think that such a way of life was suitable only for rickety old codgers like Little Morning or ancient mammies with bandannas and rheumy eyes with a bulge of snuff in their wrinkled cheeks? Certainly a boy who had learned as much as I had could not contemplate such a fruitless lifetime with anything but despondency and dread.

For a moment I was unable to answer. I do not believe that I had ever thought of the future; it is not in the mood of a Negro, once aware of the irrecoverable fact of his bondage, to dwell on the future at all, and even I in my state of relative good fortune must have simply assumed without thought that the days and years which stretched out before me would present only the familiar repetitious and interminable clutter of dirty dishes, chimney ashes, muddy boots, tarnished doorknobs, chamber pots, mops and brooms. That something *different* might befall my lot had never occurred to me. I do not know what I was about to reply when he slapped me gently on the shoulder, exclaiming in an eager, hearty voice: "I have grander plans for this young darky."

* * *

I suspect that it was a kind of loneliness, together with the fact that I had an amount of leisure not granted to many other slaves, which helped cause me at this time so zealously to precipitate myself into a study of the Bible, where I acquired—even at that early age— such a reverence and a sense of majesty in the presence of the Psalms and in the teachings of the great Prophets that I resolved that no matter where my destiny took me, no matter what humdrum tasks befell my lot in later years, I would become first and foremost a preacher of the Word. At Christmas time one year Miss made me a gift of a Bible—one of several left at Turner's by an itinerant messenger of the Bible Society in Richmond. "Heed this good book, Nathaniel," she said in her soft distant voice, "and happiness shall attend you wherever you go." I will never forget my excitement as she pressed the leather-covered Bible into my hands. Surely at that moment I must have been (though all unaware) the only black boy in Virginia who possessed a book.

My joy was so great that I became dizzy, and I began to tremble and sweat, though windy drafts swept through the house and the day was bitterly cold. I was overtaken by such a bewildering emotion that I could not even thank the good lady, but merely turned and went to my little room, where I sat on the cornshuck tick in the slanting icicle light of Christmas afternoon, quite unable to lift the cover and look at the pages. I recall the scent of cedar logs burning in the kitchen beyond the wall behind me, and the kitchen warmth stealing through the cracks of the timbers at my back. I recall too the echo of the spinet piano dimly tinkling far off in the great hall of the house and the sound of white people's voices lifted in song—*Joy to the world the Lord is come*—while with the Bible still clutched unopened in my hands I gazed through a warped and crinkled isinglass windowpane to the sere wind-swept slope outside: there a mob of Negroes from the cabins was trooping toward the house. Muffled up against the cold in the coarse and shapeless yet decent winter garments Marse Samuel provided for them, they straggled along in a single line, men, women, pickaninnies, prepared to receive their gifts—a beanbag or a hunk of rock candy for the children, a yard of calico for the women, a plug of tobacco or a cheap jackknife for the men. They were a disheveled, ragged lot, and as they clumped past on the frozen ground near the window I could hear the babble of their voices, filled with Christmas anticipation, laughter high and heedless, and loutish nigger cheer. The sight of them suddenly touched me with a loathing so intense that it was akin to disgust, bellysickness, and I turned my eyes away, throwing open the Bible at last to a passage whose meaning was lost on me then entirely but which I never forgot and now in the night of all that has since come to pass shimmers in my memory like a transfiguration: *I will ransom them from the power of the grave; I will redeem them from death: O death, I will be thy plagues; O grave, I will be thy destruction . . .*

2.

A passing wagon or cart, hours before, had run over and crushed a turtle. Margaret had spied it from her side of the buggy and she insisted—with another tug at my sleeve—that we climb down and help it, for she had seen that it was still alive. "Oh, the poor thing," she whispered as we viewed the little beast. The black and brown mosaic of the turtle's shell had been split down the center from side to side, a pale bloody paste oozed out of the fissure and from a spider-web of minute fracture marks that grooved the surf ace of the shell. Yet, indeed, the turtle still lived; it wiggled feebly and hopelessly with its outstretched legs and craned its long leathery neck and remained immobile, dying, jaws agape and hooded eyes mossed over in some dim reptilian anguish. I touched it lightly with my toe.

"Oh, the poor thing," Margaret said again.

"Ain't nothing but a turtle, missy," I said.

"Oh, but it must suffer so."

"I'll put it away," I replied.

She was silent for a moment, then said softly: "Oh yes, do."

I found a hickory branch at the side of the road and smote the head of the turtle hard, a single time; its legs and tail quivered briefly, then relaxed with a soft uncurling motion, the tail drooped, and it was dead. When I threw the stick into the field and turned back to Margaret, I saw that her lips were trembling.

"'Twasn't nothin' but an old turtle, missy," I said. "Turtle don't feel anything. He's pretty dumb. They's an old nigger sayin' about animals that goes, 'They that doesn't holler doesn't hurt.' "

"Oh, I know it's silly," she said, composing herself. "It's just—oh, suffering things." Suddenly she put her fingers to her forehead. "I'm kind of dizzy. And it's hot. Oh, I wish I could have a sip of water. I'm so thirsty."

I kicked the turtle into the ditch.

"Well, they's a brook that runs along back in those trees there," I said. "Same brook that goes by yo' mamma's place. It's fit to drink here, I know, missy. I'd fetch you some water but I don't have a thing to carry it in."

"Oh come, we'll walk," she replied.

Her spirits brightened again as I led the way across a scrubby parched field toward the stream. "I'm really very sorry that I spoke of Charlotte Tyler Saunders in that fashion," she said cheerfully behind me. "She's really just the sweetest girl. And so talented. Oh, did I ever tell you about this masque that we wrote together, Nat?"

"No, missy," I replied, "I don't believe so."

"Well, a masque is a sort of a play in verse—you spell it with a q-u-e on the end—and it's quite short and it has to do with elevated themes—oh, I mean things of the spirit and philosophy and poetical matters and such like. Anyway, we did this masque together and it was performed at the Seminary last spring. It was quite some success, I can tell you that. I mean after it was performed, do you know, Dr. Simpson told Charlotte Tyler and me that it was the equal of dramas he had seen performed up North on the stages of Philadelphia and New York. And Mrs. Simpson—that's his wife—told us that rarely if ever had she seen a performance that was so affecting and imbued with such lofty ideals. Those were her words. Anyway, this masque that we wrote is called *The Melancholy Shepherdess*. It's laid in first-century Rome. In one way it's very pagan but at the same time it exemplifies the highest aspirations of Christian belief. Anyway, there are these five characters. At the Seminary they were all played by girls, naturally. The heroine is a young shepherdess who lives on the outskirts of Rome named Celia. She is a very devout Christian. The hero is the young manor lord whose name is Philemon. He's very handsome and everything, you see, and *au fond* he's very kindly and good but his religion is still quite pagan. Actually, the truth is that his religion is animistic . . ."

As the dry field gave way to a patch of woods I could hear water splashing in the brook. The sunlight dimmed out as we entered the grove of trees; a ferny coolness enveloped me, there were pine needles underfoot and I smelled the sharp bittersweet odor of rosin. The closeness, the stillness, the seclusion here created once more a voluptuous stirring in my blood. I turned now to guide her by my glance, and for an instant her eyes met mine unflinchingly, not so much coquettish as insistent—inviting, daring, almost expecting my gaze to repose in her own eyes while she prattled blissfully on. Although as brief and fleeting as the space of a blink, it was the longest encounter I could remember ever having with a white person's eyes. Unaccountably, my heart swelled in my throat in a quick ball of fear. I turned away, swept with lust again, hating her guts, now driven close to distraction by that chattering monologue pitched at a girlish whisper which I no longer bothered to listen to or to understand. Years and decades of pine needles made a buoyant sweet-smelling carpet sibilant beneath our feet. I paused to dislodge a pine branch that lay across our path, then rose, and she gave a little murmur of surprise as the fullness of her breast bumped the flesh of my arm in soft collision. But she paid it no notice, continued talking while we walked down toward the stream. I was oblivious of her words. The place where her breast had met my arm was like an incandescence, tingling; again I was smothered by remorseless desire. Insanely, I found myself measuring the risk. *Take her,* a voice said. *(Take her here on this bank by this quiet brook. Spend upon her all afternoon a backed-up lifetime of passion. Without mercy take your pleasure upon her innocent round young body until she is half mad with fright and pain. Forget your great mission. Abandon all for these hours of terror and bliss . . .)* I felt my virile part stiffen again beneath my trousers, and I was suddenly and absurdly torn between fear that she might see my state and an impulse to expose it to her—oh God, forget it, forget it! Never could I remember having been so unhinged by desire and hatred. Trying to settle my emotions I said in an uncertain voice, too loud: "There's the water!"

"Oh, I'm so thirsty!" she exclaimed. Fallen trees made a little rapids here, and the water foamed over the logs cool and green. I watched as she knelt by the brook and brought pale cupfuls of water up to her face in the curved hollow of her hands. Now, the voice said, *take her now.*

"Oh, that's better!" she said, drawing back. "Don't you want some, Nat?" And without waiting for an answer, went on: "Anyway, Nat, after this wicked Fidessa kills herself in remorse, then Philemon takes his sword and kills Pactolus, the evil old soothsayer. I played Philemon in our performance and that part was such fun, I mean with wooden swords and all. Then Philemon is converted to Christianity by Celia and in the very last scene you see them as they plight their troth. And then there are these last lines, I mean what is known on the stage as curtain speeches. That's where Philemon holds his sword up in front of Celia like a cross and says: *e'll love one another by the light of heaven above . . ."*

Margaret rose from her knees and turned, standing at the edge of the brook with her arms outstretched to the air, transfigured as if before a crowd of onlookers, her eyes half closed. "Then Celia says: *Oh, I* would fain *swoon* into an *eternity of love!*

"Curtain! That's all!" she said brightly, proudly, looking toward me. "Isn't that a wonderful masque? I mean it has a very poetical, religious quality, even if I do say so myself."

I made no reply, but now as she moved from the side of the stream she tripped, gave a little cry, and for the briefest instant fell against me, clasping my arms with her still-wet hands. I grabbed her about the shoulders—only as if to prevent her falling—and as quickly let her go, but not so quickly that in the intervening space I did not smell her skin and her closeness and feel the electric passage across my cheek of strands of chestnut-colored hair. During that moment I heard her breathing and our eyes met in a wayward glint of light that seemed to last much longer than any mere glance exchanged between two strangers journeying of a summer afternoon to some drowsy dwelling far off in the country.

Could it be, too, that I felt her relax, go the faintest bit limp, as she slumped against me? This I would never know, for swiftly we were apart; a cloud passed over the day, bringing shadows and a breeze which teased the loosened, wanton edges of her hair. The flicker of an instant then, no more, but she was frozen in an attitude of stiff, still death. As the wind rose there was a clatter in the trees like the noise of cataclysmic strife, and I was suddenly—without reason—inconsolable with an emptiness such as I have never known.

Then she trembled as if with a chill, saying gently, "We'd better hurry back, Nat." And I, walking beside her now, replied, "Yes, missy," and this was the last time—but for one—that I ever looked into her face.

3.

On foot now I skirted Richard Whitehead's corpse lying face down between two rows of cotton. I walked unsteadily, following along the old familiar log fence which I myself had helped build, separating field and barnyard. My men in the house, in the stable, and in the barn, were making a barbaric racket. Still more screams erupted from the house: I remembered that Mrs. Whitehead's summer-visiting daughters were home. I clambered over the fence, nearly falling. As I grabbed for the post, I glimpsed the gross old house nigger Hubbard, at gunpoint, being forced into a wagon by Henry and another: captive eunuch, he would not go with us willingly, but tied up in the cart with other pet collected coons, would surely go. "Lawd, sweet Lawd!" he boohooed to the skies as they shoved him up into the wagon, and he sobbed as if his heart would perish. At that moment I rounded the corner of the oxen barn and looked toward the porch of the house. There deserted of all save those two acting out their final tableau— the tar-black man and the woman, bone-white, bone-rigid with fear beyond telling, pressed urgently together against the door in a simulacrum of shattered oneness and heartsick farewell—the porch seemed washed for an instant in light that flowed from the dawn of my own beginning. Then I saw Will draw back as if from a kiss and with a swift sideways motion nearly decapitate Mrs. Whitehead in a single stroke.

And he had seen me. "Dar she is, preacher man, dey's one left!" he howled. "An' she all your'n! Right by de cellah do'! Go git her, preacher man!" he taunted me in his wild rage. "If'n you cain't make de red juice run you cain't run de army!"

Soundless, uttering not a word, Margaret Whitehead rose up and scrambled from her hiding place beyond the sheltering wall of the cellar door and fled me—fled me like the wind. Fleet and light she ran, after the fashion of a child, with bare arms stiffly outstretched, brown hair tied with a bow and tossing this way and that above a blue taffeta dress, pressed to her back in a sweaty oblong of deeper blue. I had not caught sight of her face and realized it was she only when, disappearing around the corner of the house, the silk ribbon which I had seen before fell from her hair and rippled briefly on the air before fluttering to earth.

"Dar! She gone!" Will roared, gesturing with his broadax to the other Negroes, who had begun to straggle across the yard. "Does you want her, preacher man, or she fo' me?"

Ah, how I want her, I thought, and unsheathed my sword. She had run into the hayfield, and when I too rounded the corner of the house I thought she had slipped away, for there was no one in sight. But she had merely fallen down in the waist-high grass and as I stood there she rose again—a small and slender figure in the distance—and

resumed her flight toward a crooked far-off fence. I ran headlong into
the field. The air was alive with grasshoppers: they skimmed and flick-
ered across my path, brushed my skin with brittle momentary sting. I
felt the sweat streaming into my eyes. The sword in my right hand
hung like the weight of all the earth. Yet I gained on Margaret quickly,
for she had tired fast, and I reached her just as she was trying to clam-
ber over the rotted pole fence. She made no sound, uttered no word,
did not turn to plead or contend or resist or even wonder. Nor did I
speak—our last encounter may have been the quietest that ever was.
Beneath her foot one of the poles gave way in crunching powdery col-
lapse and she tripped forward, bare arms still outthrust as if to welcome someone beloved and long-unseen. As she stumbled thus, then
recovered, I heard for the first time her hurtful, ragged breathing, and
it was with this sound in my ears that I plunged the sword into her
side, just below and behind her breast. She screamed then at last.
Litheness, grace, the body's nimble felicity—all fled her like ghosts.
She crumpled to earth, limp, a rag, and as she fell I stabbed her again
in the same place, or near it, where pulsing blood already encrim-
soned the taffeta's blue. There was no scream this time although the
echo of the first sang in my ears like a far angelic cry; when I turned
aside from her fallen body I was troubled by a steady soughing noise
like the rise and fall of a summer tempest in a grove of pines and realized that it was the clamor of my own breathing as it welled up in
sobs from my chest.

I lurched away from her through the field, calling out to myself like
one bereft of mind. Yet hardly had I taken a dozen steps when I heard
her voice, weak, frail, almost without breath, not so much voice as
memory—faint as if from some distant and half-forgotten lawn of
childhood: Oh Nat I hurt so. Please kill me. Nat I hurt so.

I stopped and looked back. "*Die*, God damn your white soul," I
wept. "Die!"

Oh Nat please kill me. I hurt so.

"Die! Die! Die! Die!"

The sword fell from my hand. I returned to her side and looked
down. Her head was cradled against the inside of her arm, as if she
had composed herself for sleep, and all the chestnut streaming luxuri-
ance of her hair had fallen in a tangle amid the hayfield's parched and
fading green. Grasshoppers stitched and stirred in restless fidget
among the weeds, darting about her face.

"I hurt so," I heard her whisper.

"Shut your eyes," I said. I reached down to search with my fingers
for a firm length of fence rail and I could sense once more her close

girl-smell and the fragrance of lavender, bitter in my nostrils, and sweet. "Shut your eyes," I told her quickly. Then when I raised the rail above her head she gazed at me, as if past the imponderable vista of her anguish, with a grave and drowsy tenderness such as I had never known, spoke some words too soft to hear and, saying no more, closed her eyes upon all madness, illusion, error, dream, and strife. So I brought the timber down and she was swiftly gone, and I hurled the hateful, shattered club far up into the weeds.

For how long I aimlessly circled her body—prowled around the corners of the field in haphazard quest for nothing, like some roaming dog—how long this went on I do not recollect. The sun rose higher, boiling; my own flesh was incandescent, and when at the farm I heard the men call for me their voices were untold distances away. By the edge of the woods I found myself seated on a log, head in my hands, unaccountably thinking of ancient moments of childhood—warm rain, leaves, a whippoorwill, rushing mill wheels, jew's harp strumming—centuries before. Then I rose again and resumed my meaningless and ordained circuit of her body, not near it yet ever within sight as if that crumpled blue were the center of an orbit around whose path I must make a ceaseless pilgrimage. And once in my strange journey I thought I heard again her whispery voice, thought I saw her rise from the blazing field with arms outstretched as if to a legion of invisible onlookers, her brown hair and innocent school gown teased by the wind as she cried: "Oh, I would fain swoon into an eternity of love!" But then she vanished before my eyes—melted instantly like an image carved of air and light—and I turned away at last and went back to join my men.

A White Scholar's Response

William Styron's novel about Nat Turner became more than a best-seller; it touched a sensitive spot in the American civil rights debate; it provoked a storm of protest. Both black and white readers took it to be a commentary on slavery and on the nature of black males. Nat Turner, the man and the image, could still in the 1960s cause controversy. Most whites who read the book praised it. Typical of that praise is the following review of Styron's novel, written for *New Republic* magazine by C. Vann Woodward. Woodward, a noted historian of the South, author of the classic study *The Burden of Southern History,* called *The Confessions of Nat Turner* "the most

profound fictional treatment of slavery in our literature." He spoke
for much of the white scholarly world when he wrote:

In the annals of American slavery two figures stand out with unrivaled
prominence among the very few who resorted to armed rebellion—John
Brown and Nat Turner, one white and one black. The historical importance of their roles is roughly comparable and there is as much reason
for enduring curiosity about the one as about the other. Of the two,
Turner's rebellion was far more bloody, both in the lives it took and in
the reprisals it evoked. As a threat to the security of a slave based society,
Turner's conspiracy was more momentous than Brown's. John Brown's
Raid never had the remotest chance of success.

Yet there is a remarkable disparity in the amount that is known and
in what has been written about the two men and their deeds. On John
Brown there exists a vast library, forty-odd biographies, massive mono-
graphs, scores of poems, plays, and works of fiction. This is partly
explained by the relative abundance of source materials. Brown left
extensive (though misleading) accounts of himself and a large mass of
correspondence. He was acquainted with some of the most prominent
writers of his day. A few intellectuals were personally involved and
many were passionately interested in his conspiracy and left their own
records. Two congressional hearings and a mountain of archival material multiply the sources.

In striking contrast, the sources on Nat Turner and the scholarly as
well as creative writing about him are minuscule. Since there were no
white participants in the rebellion and the life of no white witness of
the massacres was spared by the rebels, the information about the
conspiracy boils down largely to twenty-odd pages of Turner's "Confessions" in the stilted prose of the Virginia lawyer to whom he dictated them in prison. Mainly on this and on a pedestrian monograph
or two rests all we know of the only slave rebellion of consequence in
the largest slave society in the 19th-century world.

If there were ever a free hand for a novelist, this was it. Yet the
obstacles were formidable. There were no models. The only major
American novelist to treat a slave rebellion was Melville, and *Benito
Cereno* is viewed entirely through the eyes of the white man. Nat's
story would have to be seen from behind the black mask. That was
the boldest decision William Styron made. There was little to go on
beyond the author's imagination. What history tells us about slavery
is mainly the white man's experience, not the black man's—what it
was like to *have* slaves, not what it was like to *be* slaves. No one has
more than an ill-informed guess about why the greatest slave republic

in the New World had by far the fewest rebellions; why smaller and allegedly more benevolent slave societies bred vast insurrections, blood baths involving many thousands of slaves that lasted scores of years, and America had one that recruited seventy-five and petered out in three days; why servility and submission were the rule and Sambo the stereotype and heritage of American slavery. And most of all, what explains the terrible enigma of Nat Turner, the other-worldly young carpenter of obscure origins and apocalyptic visions who at the age of thirty-one took the road to Jerusalem, Virginia, martyrdom, and immortality.

To complicate the enigma, the rebellion took place not in the brutal Delta cotton fields or the Louisiana sugar cane, but in mellowed, impoverished tidewater Virginia, where even Nat Turner thought there was "still an ebb and flow of human sympathy—no matter how strained and imperfect—between slave and master." And Nat himself was a product of benevolent, if unusual, paternalism at its best— fondly educated, trained in a craft, and promised liberation. The picture of Nat's life and motivation the novelist constructs is, but for a few scraps of evidence, without historical underpinnings, but most historians would agree, I think, not inconsistent with anything historians know. It is informed by a respect for history, a sure feeling for the period, and a deep and precise sense of place and time.

Nat was the child of a house servant and grew up in the big house, familiar with "the chink of silver and china" as well as his "black Negro world" of the kitchen, but not with the toil of field and mill. His mistress taught him to read and gave him a Bible, of which he learned great parts by heart and knew better than the white preachers of the parish. He discovered his intelligence and his ability to charm, grew accustomed to love from all sides, and never encountered harshness or brutality. "I became in short a pet, the darling, the little black jewel of Turner's Mill. Pampered, fondled, nudged, pinched, I was the household's spoiled child." Toward his master, Samuel Turner, he felt a regard "very close to the feeling one should bear only toward the Divinity." Between them were "strong ties of emotion," in fact, "a kind of love." The master responded by giving encouragement, careful training, flattering responsibilities, and, three years before Nat came of age, the intoxicating promise of freedom. Toward the field hands beyond the big house perimeter little Nat felt a contemptuous disdain, regarding them as "a lower order of people—a ragtag mob, coarse, raucous, clownish, uncouth." He identified completely with his master and looking back later realized that had this life continued he would have achieved in old age "a kind of purse-lipped dignity, known as Uncle Nat, well loved and adoring in return, a palsied stroker of the silken pates of little white grandchildren."

But that life came to an end when Samuel Turner went bankrupt and moved to Alabama when Nat was twenty. Before leaving Virginia he placed Nat in the care of a poverty-ravaged, fanatical Baptist preacher under legal obligation to free his charge in a stated time. Instead, after giving Nat a year's taste of how degrading slavery could be, the preacher sold him for $460 to an illiterate brute named Moore, from whom he eventually passed into the hands of his late owner, Travis. Among the many harsh lessons these experiences taught Nat was "how greatly various were the moral attributes of white men who possessed slaves, how different each owner might be by way of severity or benevolence." They ranged "from the saintly," such as his first owner, "to a few who were unconditionally monstrous." Nat never fell into the hands of the last type, and his owner at the time of the rebellion generally behaved "like every slave's ideal master." Whatever accounts for Nat's rebellion, it was not the irrepressible rage of the intolerably oppressed. Instead, he observed, "the more tolerable and human white people became in their dealings with me, the keener was my passion to destroy them."

Nat was twenty and on the threshold of freedom before he suddenly realized what slavery was, "the *true* world in which a Negro moves and breathes. It was like being plunged into freezing water." A year later came his betrayal, the final shattering of the dream of freedom, and his submission to a master he knew to be his moral inferior, stupid, brutal, swinish. For nearly ten years his disciplined defense was to become "a paragon of rectitude, of alacrity, of lively industriousness, of sweet equanimity and uncomplaining obedience," the ideal slave. He had learned never to look a white man in the eye, how to smell danger, how like a dog "to interpret the *tone* of what is being said," how to assume "that posture of respect and deference it is wise for any Negro to assume" in the presence of a strange white man, and how to "emerge faceless and nameless with the common swarm." He learned how, when necessary, to shuffle and scrape and adopt the egregious, gluey cornfield accents and postures of niggerness.

He became a discriminating connoisseur of Sambo types, those given to "wallowing in the dust at the slightest provocation, midriffs clutched in idiot laughter," those who "endear themselves to all, white and black, through droll interminable tales about ha'nts and witches and conjures," and at the other extreme those who "reverse this procedure entirely and in *their* niggerness are able to outdo many white people in presenting to the world a grotesque swagger," a posture suited to the black driver or the tyrannical kitchen mammy and butler, who were skilled in keeping "safely this side of insolence." For his own part, Nat "decided upon humility, a soft voice, and houndlike obedience." Yet he was always conscious of "the weird unnaturalness of this adopted role," always counseling himself "to patience, patience, *patience* to the end," biding his time.

As he watched the potential recruits for his divine mission of vengeance and liberation he often despaired. His black brothers, "half drowned from birth in a kind of murky mindlessness," drifted before him "mouths agape or with sloppy uncomprehending smiles, shuffling their feet." They would suddenly seem to him "as meaningless and as stupid as a barnful of mules," and he would "hate them one and all." But this hatred would alternate with "a kind of wild, desperate love for them." The ambivalence came out in his feelings about Hark (originally named Hercules) whom he intended to make one of his lieutenants. Hark had "the face of an African chieftain," a god-like frame and strength, and a mortal grievance against his master for selling his wife and child. "Yet the very sight of white skin cowed him, humbled him to the most servile abasement." He drove Nat to incoherent rage when in the presence of any white he unconsciously became "the unspeakable bootlicking Sambo, all giggles and smirks and oily, sniveling servility." Hark's defense was that he was overcome by "dat black-assed feelin'," and Nat admitted to himself that the expression perfectly expressed "the numbness and dread which dwells in every Negro's heart."

Nat labored desperately to quell this fear in his recruits and to instill pride and confidence and blind faith in their leader. He clung to his faith that in every Sambo was a Nat Turner, that while "most Negroes are hopelessly docile, many of them are filled with fury," and that servility was "but a form of self-preservation." In the more desperate of them he counted upon the common postulate that "nigger life ain't worth pig shit"—they had nothing to lose.

It is one mark of William Styron's genius that he deliberately threw away the Christ symbol, which would have been irresistible to many novelists. For Nat was strictly Old Testament, the stuff of Ezekiel, Daniel, Isaiah, and Jeremiah, the blood-stained righteousness of his somber Hebrew heroes, Joshua and David. He thought and spoke in the rhetoric of the Prophets and the Psalms and scriptural poetry weaves in and out of his ruminations. He fasted and prayed in the wilderness and waited for a sign. And the sign came: "Then swiftly in the very midst of the rent in the clouds I saw a black angel clothed in black armor with black wings outspread from east to west; gigantic, hovering, he spoke in a thunderous voice louder than anything I had ever heard: *'Fear God and give glory to Him for the hour of His judgment is come . . .'.*"

Against the hour of the bloodbath Nat had steeled himself in apocalyptic hatred, "hatred so pure and obdurate that no sympathy, no human warmth, no flicker of compassion can make the faintest nick or scratch upon the stony surface of its being." He had achieved this exaltation, he thought, by "knowing the white man at close hand," by becoming "knowledgeable about the white man's wiles, his duplicity, his greediness, and his ultimate depravity," and most of all by "having submitted to his wanton and arrogant kindness." Then when the moment came and the dread axe was poised over his master's head, Nat's hand palsied and the blow missed. Again and again between violent seizures of vomiting he tried to kill and failed. Initiative fell to a demented black monster maddened by a master's brutality. The only life Nat was able to take, among the scores slaughtered, was that of the one white person he still loved, a simple-hearted and sympathetic girl.

This is the most profound fictional treatment of slavery in our literature. It is, of course, the work of a skilled and experienced novelist with other achievements to attest his qualifications. It is doubtful, however, if the rare combination of talents essential to this formidable undertaking, a flawless command of dialect, a native instinct for the subtleties and ambivalences of race in the South, and a profound and unerring sense of place—Styron's native place as it was Nat Turner's—could well have been found anywhere else.

A BLACK SCHOLAR'S RESPONSE

Woodward was not alone in his praise of Styron's achievement. The book went on to win a Pulitzer Prize for fiction. Most of the reviewers who approved of Styron's Nat Turner, both the book and the image of the insurrectionist, were white; but a few were black, including the critic Saunders Redding, the distinguished historian John Hope Franklin, and the novelist James Baldwin. Baldwin, in fact, saw a bit of himself in Styron's Nat: a shy black boy preacher who had been anointed to liberate his people. "This is the beginning of our common history," he wrote of *The Confessions.*

A new, different breeze of black opinion was rising, however, and slowly the voices of dissenters began to make themselves heard. "Truth squads" of black critics disrupted Styron's appearances at literary and historical meetings. Styron's Nat Turner was to these younger black spokesmen the typical white man's fantasy: a meek black celibate whose only sexual experience had been with another boy, a religious fanatic driven to homicidal violence by his desire for a white girl. The younger generation found Styron's Nat Turner a false and demeaning symbol of black manhood. Lerone Bennett Jr., then a senior editor at *Ebony* magazine, decried Styron's re-creation of what he called "Big Black Sambo." Styron, Bennett concluded, demonstrated in his novel the way "white Americans use black Americans, no matter what we do. When we refrain from cutting throats, they stigmatize us as bootlicking Sambos. And when we cut throats, they make us a Book-of-the-Month-Club selection. . . ."

Perhaps the most perceptive and articulate of the outraged black intellectuals who condemned Styron's Nat Turner was New England psychiatrist Dr. Alvin Poussaint. In the following commentary on the novel he emphasizes what he considers the debilitating dilemma of white author William Styron as he tried to portray a black hero:

The Confessions of Nat Turner by William Styron would be more appropriately titled: "The *Imaginations* of William Styron on the Life of Nat Turner." The author himself, in a note at the beginning of his book, states, ". . . in those areas where there is little knowledge in regard to Nat, his early life, and the motivations for the revolt (and such knowledge is lacking most of the time), I have allowed myself the *utmost freedom of imagination* in reconstructing events . . ." [Emphasis added]. No one objects to a novelist using the best of his imagination to write a work of fiction that will have color and saleability. However, Styron is a southern white man who has been raised in a racist society and is not free from the impact of its teachings. How will we ever know how well the author has freed himself of his own white supremacist attitudes as he attempts to project himself into the mind of a black slave?

In the author's note quoted above Styron refers to Nat Turner simply as "Nat." Is this familiarity by the author part of intuitive white condescension and adherence to southern racial etiquette? Is this reference and the entire book an unconscious attempt to keep Nat Turner "in his place"—to emasculate him? Would the novelist expect Nat Turner to address him as "Mr. Styron"? Perhaps no one can ever know the answers to these questions. Yet, they are raised to indicate the potentially profound difficulties that are inherent in Styron's undertaking.

It seems to me that Styron may be guilty of projecting on to Nat Turner many of the classical white stereotypical notions about black people. I am not suggesting that Styron intentionally wished to malign the character and historical significance of Nat Turner. However, through his "imaginations" he unwittingly has selected the types of psychological material which appear to emasculate and degrade Nat Turner and his people. In so doing, the author must accept the responsibility for whatever part his book will play in perpetuating the racist myth of our white society. Since this book has been dubbed an "historical novel" many of the readers will accept the author's "freedom of imagination" as "fact." Thus, the psychological impact on the American public of this widely publicized literary work will be considerable.

For me, *The Confessions of Nat Turner* seems to reveal some obvious and some subtle manifestations of white racist attitudes.

First, almost all of the important and influential persons in our protagonist's early developmental years were white. Even Nat Turner's mother is given a secondary and insignificant role. Instead, those who are portrayed as being most crucial are "Miss Nell, Miss Emmeline, and Marse Samuel." All the people he seemed to "worship" were white. Were there no influential or worthy black people in his life? From the standpoint of current psychological theory one would expect that whatever greatness and strength of character Nat Turner possessed would stem primarily from his early rearing with his mother and father (who are scarcely considered in the book). Yet, the wanderings of Styron's mind seem to focus mainly on his relations with white people. Is this because of a commonly held racist view that a Negro who achieves must be primarily doing so because of his associations with whites? This somewhat disguised theme of "white is right" can be seen in other basic aspects of *The Confessions*.

For example, Nat Turner as a character seems to be quite white. His speech sounds more like Styron's than that of an heroic black slave of nineteenth-century America. In fact, in many places the writer's "imagination" seems to run wild. For example, here is Styron's Nat Turner as he waits on a deserted plantation, "Now looking down at the shops and barns and cabins and distant fields, I was no longer the grinning black boy in velvet pantaloons; for a fleeting moment instead I owned all, and so exercised the privilege of ownership by unlacing my fly and pissing loudly on the same worn stone where dainty tiptoeing feet had gained the veranda steps a short three years before. What a strange, demented ecstasy! How white I was! What wicked joy!" [page 232]. Is this really our black protagonist speaking, or are we witnessing some sort of vicarious and prurient joy which Styron experiences by projecting this type of imagery into the mind of Nat Turner?

Our hero is also portrayed as a "house nigger" possessing the full range of currently popular and usually overgeneralized feelings of self-hatred, anti-Negro attitudes and a desire to be white which psychiatrists tell us plague black people in a racist culture. However, Nat Turner was a unique and great individual. It could be that what really distinguished him was the fact that he was not indoctrinated with the psyche of a "house nigger." It is just as reasonable, from a psychological viewpoint, to speculate that he did not hate his blackness and that it was self-love that made him a revolutionist revolting against the abominable institution of slavery. There is certainly little in the original confessions of Nat Turner which suggest that he ever played the psychological role of a "house nigger" or "Uncle Tom." Styron's reconstruction of events is an example of the stereotyped belief that black people rebel primarily because of an unfulfilled psychological need to be white and not because of a sense of their own inner dignity. This notion, of course, is the self-flattery of the oppressor who cannot imagine that a black man could want to be anything unless it is an emulation of himself.

And, it follows naturally that if the black man cannot be like the white man then he must certainly yearn for the white woman with an erotic-religious fervor which implies that salvation itself must lie in her loins. This idea is another major psychological theme of *The Confessions*. Once again, Styron presents a Caucasian stereotype of the black man's innermost desires, which is to sexually possess a white woman. This is what the white racists have been telling the black man for centuries. It was the theme of the great racist classic, *The Birth of a Nation*, which glorified the Ku Klux Klan. Therefore, it is not surprising that Styron might sense its appeal to a primarily white American audience.

Why does the author choose to depict Nat Turner as a celibate pining for white women? There is at least one historical account which indicates that he was married to a black slave girl. In the original *Confessions* there is nothing to suggest that our protagonist or his followers were desirous of sexually possessing white female flesh! In fact, Turner and his troops did not sexually molest or rape any white woman whom they had slain or encountered. As anyone acquainted with the behavior of conquering soldiers will testify, this is amazing self-restraint for a band of "drunken" and "undisciplined" black troops. Why didn't these white-women-hungry slaves take advantage of their opportunity? Why does Styron in his tale go so far in distorting the actual historical facts?

The author takes the one recorded fact, that the only person Nat Turner actually killed himself was Miss Margaret Whitehead, and uses this to spin an enormous tale of Turner's overwhelming, erotic, and quasi-religious attachment to this young girl and her "whiteness." In the novel, even as Nat Turner is going to his death he is still languishing for her white body. In fact, the writer makes it appear as if our black rebel's strength and wish to revolt somehow stemmed mainly from his associations (both real and fantasied) with Miss Margaret. On the last page of the novel as Turner is being led to his execution he is quoted as saying, ". . . I would have done it all again. I would have destroyed them all. Yet I would have spared one. I would have spared *her that showed me Him* whose presence I had not fathomed or maybe never even known" [Emphasis added]. It is clear that from this passage and from others throughout the novel, Styron feels that Nat Turner's emotional attachment to this white "forbidden fruit" was a key factor in his psychological motivation.

Once again we see propagated the hackneyed racist belief that Negroes who are strong, successful, and masculine must also want to possess a white woman in order to give final sanction to their manhood. Why is not the author able to "imagine" that Nat Turner had a young, feminine, beautiful, and courageous black woman who stood by his side throughout his heroic plan to revolt against slavery!?

I think Styron's selection of "factual" and psychological material speaks for itself. It speaks for itself again when we read that the closest our black rebel comes to a realized sexual experience is through a homosexual one with another young black slave. What is the communication here? Naturally, it implies that Nat Turner was not a man at all. It suggests that he was unconsciously really feminine. Styron underscores this image by depicting Turner as a bungling, awkward soldier who is unable to kill his oppressors and pukes at the sight of blood during combat. Thus, throughout the book he is revealed as an emasculated and "abnormal" character. There is even the suggestion here that the rebellion was participated in reluctantly by the "sensitive" Nat Turner who really only wished to sleep with Miss Margaret to salvage his manhood. The depiction of the young rebel as a would-be deviant carries the implication that the whole revolt against slavery and racism was somehow illegitimate and "abnormal." The author on some level must realize the implications of presenting this type of psychological material to his readers.

I am puzzled as to why Styron in his "imaginations" found it necessary to degrade and emasculate the character of Nat Turner. I have no reason to believe that this was his conscious intention, for in many parts of the novel I detect a strong empathy which the author has for his protagonist. In his foreword to the book he writes, ". . . it has been my own intention to try to re-create a man and his era . . ." Yet, given the facts and content of the novel, one wonders if Styron was an unwitting victim of his own unconscious white racism for which he alone can not be held fully accountable.

QUESTIONS FOR RESPONSIVE ESSAYS

1. Keeping in mind that William Styron's book is fiction, discuss "Nat's" relationship with "Margaret." How much of his attraction to her was cultural, and how much was sexual? Can the two be separated? What cultural conditioning blinded "Margaret" to how she provoked "Nat"? What can be said about a slave society that both encouraged and prohibited such attraction?

2. The literary critic George Core scoffed at black criticism of Styron's portrayal of Nat Turner, saying that Indians never found such fault with Englishman E. M. Forster's *A Passage to India.* Argue whether you do or do not think that a white Virginian could honestly and correctly tell the story of an African-American slave.

3. William Styron himself commented that if a black writer had written *Nat Turner* "he would have become the most celebrated black writer in history and the most loved by blacks." Is this statement true or false? What *Nat Turner* would a black novelist have created?

4. Explaining his thesis that "Nat" killed "Margaret" because he loved her, Styron once said, "I had to plunge into some sort of psychological state in order to achieve the kind of insight I did." What are the pitfalls of trying, without training in psychology, to analyze historical figures in this way, especially a figure like Nat Turner, especially by a writer of Styron's background? To what extent can such plunging into a psychological state help a writer tell an accurate story, and to what extent can it create mere fantasy? Is psychological fiction helpful to students of history?

SUGGESTED TOPICS FOR ESSAYS AND PAPERS

1. Use the example of Nat Turner to demonstrate how one person can strongly affect the way a nation thinks about a specific issue. What made Turner such a person? What exactly is his influence on the American Mind? What will his influence be in the future?

2. What was Nat Turner's short- and long-term affect on other slaves? How did they react and respond to his insurrection? Were their actions better than his, short-term and long-term?

3. Show how Nat Turner's image changed over time and what he meant to people in each time period from 1831 to the present. How do each of Turner's various images reflect the hopes and fears of Americans of various races in each of these periods?

4. Use Nat Turner, his uprising, and the effect it had on American history to argue one side of the age-old historical question: Does the end justify the means? Was Turner justified in what he did, even if in the short-term he failed? Did slave owners and the slave society deserve his action? Was he foolhardy or just ahead of his time?

SELECTED BIBLIOGRAPHY FOR A PAPER ON NAT TURNER

Books

Bontemps, Arna Wendell. *Great Slave Narratives*. Boston: Beacon Press, 1969. This is a wonderful collection of stories, providing a graphic picture of what life was like when slavery existed in America.

Clarke, J.H. (ed). *William Styron's Nat Turner: Ten Black Writers Respond*. Boston: Beacon Press, 1968. All ten of these black writers, including Alvin Poussaint, reject what they consider the racist portrayal of Turner by Styron.

Douglass, Frederick. *My Bondage and My Freedom*. Many editions are available. Well written and timeless, it is must reading for an understanding of the personal dynamics of slavery.

Foner, Eric. *Nat Turner*. Englewood, N.J.: Prentice-Hall, 1971. An excellent survey of opinions about the Turner Rebellion. Because of its publication date, it does not contain the very latest interpretations, but it puts Nat Turner in excellent historical context.

Jacobs, Harriet A. *Incidents in the Life of a Slave Girl*. Cambridge: Harvard University Press, 1987. This is the entire story of Jacobs' flight from slavery, excellently prepared and vividly presented.

Johnson, Frank Roy. *The Nat Turner Story*. Murphreesboro, N.C.: Johnson Publishing Company, 1970. An interesting survey of popular myths which have grown up around the insurrection and its leader.

Olmsted, Frederick Law. *The Cotton Kingdom*. (First published in 1861, here edited by Arthur Schlessinger). New York: Alfred A. Knopf, 1953. This is the story of a visitor to the slave south before the Civil War, and its portrait of the society there informs one of the life Nat Turner would have lived in slavery.

Stone, Albert E. *The Return of Nat Turner*. Athens: University of Georgia Press, 1992. A study of the Styron novel and the arguments it raised. It features an appendix containing the original transcript of Turner's "Confession" to Gray.

Styron, William. *The Confessions of Nat Turner*. New York: Random House, 1966. The Pulitzer Prize winning novel, which raised the issue of Nat Turner for a new generation and caused such controversy.

Tragle, Henry Irving. *The Southampton Slave Revolt of 1831*. Amherst: University of Massachusetts Press, 1971. One of the best source texts for newspaper articles, documents, and chronology of events surrounding the insurrection. It also provides more interpretation of events than most books.

Articles

Aptheker, Herbert. ". . . A Note on the History." *Nation* (October 16, 1967): 375-376. Aptheker, a Marxist by political persuasion, takes issue with many of William Styron's facts in the novel, *The Confessions of Nat Turner*. Having written his own book on the Turner uprising, Aptheker believes Styron's portrayal of Turner is a caricature. In the April 22, 1968 edition of this journal, Aptheker and Styron exchange views—quite entertaining, but in the end remaining at odds.

Mayer, Henry. "The Fires of Jubilee." *New York Times Book Review* (October 5, 1975): 12. This is a strong review of Stephen B. Oates' book by the same name on the Turner uprising. Mayer acknowledges the accuracy of Oates' treatment but criticizes the book for presenting too unemotional a story. Mayer believes that Nat Turner cannot be approached in a neutral, rational way.

Oates, Stephen B. "Styron and the Blacks—Another View." *Nation* (May 31, 1975): 662-664. This is an abbreviated version of the book Oates was then about to publish on the Turner uprising, *The Fires of Jubilee*. He tries here to demonstrate that his book will be a historical study, not the historical fiction of William Styron.

Schroth, Raymond A. "Nat Turner's Sword." *America* (October 14, 1967): 416. One of the earliest reviews of the Styron novel, it reflects the first response by the white press: a positive, laudatory opinion which was soon to be challenged by minorities.

Styron, William. "Nat Turner Revisited." *American Heritage* (October, 1992): 64-73. Twenty-five years after the publication of his controversial novel on Nat Turner, Styron writes about the experience of being labeled a racist for his book's treatment of this historical figure. Yet he is unapologetic, saying that he was a victim of a sudden shift in public opinion which he could not have foreseen.

Woodward, C. Vann. "Confessions of a Rebel: 1831." *New Republic* (October 7, 1967): 25-28. This is the article reviewing Styron's novel by the respected historian which is included in this book. It might be helpful to compare it to a radio interview Woodward and R. W. B. Lewis had with Styron, published in the *Yale (University) Alumni Magazine* (November, 1967), pp. 33-39.

Credits and Acknowledgments

Text

Excerpts from *The Fires of Jubilee* by Stephen B. Oates, pp. 21–22, 24–26, 27–28, 31–32. © 1975 by Stephen B. Oates. Reprinted by permission of HarperCollins Publishers, Inc.

Excerpts from *The Confessions of Nat Turner* by William Styron. © 1966, 1967 by William Styron. Reprinted by permission of Random House, Inc.

Excerpts from "Confessions of a Rebel" by C. Vann Woodward reprinted by permission of *The New Republic,* © 1967, The New Republic, Inc.

Excerpts from "Dilemma of William Styron" by Alvin Poussaint in *William Styron's Nat Turner,* Boston: Beacon Press, 1968. Reprinted by permission of the author.

Photos

p. xii... *The Southampton Slave Revolt of 1831,* © 1971 by Henry Irving Tragle, from a print used in contemporary newspapers, with source listed as "unknown." University of Massachusetts Press.

p. 7..... Culver Pictures.

p. 22... Courtesy of James Weldon Johnson Memorial Collection of Negro Arts and Letters, Beinecke Library, Yale University.

p. 30... Culver Pictures.

p. 34... *The Southampton Slave Revolt of 1831,* © 1971 by Henry Irving Tragle, University of Massachusetts Press.

INDEX